LST 388

A WORLD WAR II JOURNAL

LST 388

ROBERT von der OSTEN
with **BARBARA von der OSTEN**

TDSS PUBLISHING
A division of The Divine Saga Studios, LLC

Copyright © 2018 Barbara von der Osten

All rights reserved. No part of this book may be reproduced in any form or by any electronic or mechanical means, including information storage and retrieval systems, without permission in writing from the authors, except by a reviewer who may quote brief passages in a review.

Originally published by Deeds Publishing, October 2017
First TDSS Publishing edition, March 2018

TDSS Publishing is a division of The Divine Saga Studios, LLC.
www.thedivinesagastudios.net

Cover design by Mark Babcock
Text design and composition by John Reinhardt Book Design

Library of Congress Cataloging-in-Publications data is available upon request.
ISBN: 978-1-7321664-0-0
Second Edition, 2018

Books are available in quantity for promotional or premium use.
For information, email info@tdsspublishing.com

10 9 8 7 6 5 4 3 2 1

For Kyler, Anja, Catherine, Danny, Robert, Margaret, and Michael

May you always have
FAIR WINDS and FOLLOWING SEAS

Contents

Preface ix
Acknowledgments xi
Foreword xiii
Author's Note xv
Introduction 1

PART I
I JOIN THE NAVY

I Join the Navy 11
Boot Camp 13
U.S. Naval Radio Training School 19
Amphibious Force Training Base 23
U.S. Naval Amphibious Training Base 31

PART II
USS *LST-388*

A Guide to Ship Acronyms Used in this Book 39
USS *LST-388* 41
The Long Voyage Across the Atlantic 51
Gibraltar 57

CONTENTS

North Africa and the Mediterranean 61

Invasion of Sicily. 73

Invasion at Salerno. 85

Last Days in North Africa. 103

Voyage to England. 113

The Long Wait 119

D-Day: The Invasion of France. 135

Channel Crossings 155

The Long Voyage Home. 169

The Atomic Bomb. 173

The USS *LST-388* After I Left 175

Epilogue 179

SEA FEVER. 195

Sources—Reading List 197

Endnotes 199

Photographs/Maps. 201

About the Authors. 203

Preface

ON A COLD, windy November day in 1984, I climbed out of a van full of photographers, stylists, and fashion models. It was to be a photo shoot, and the location was Normandy on the northern coast of France. Young and naïve, all I simply knew was that my Dad had been here as part of the US Navy during World War II.

The details wouldn't be revealed to me until ten years later, in 1994, when I volunteered to re-type my Dad's WWII journals, after they had lovingly been compiled by him and my Mom. From that point on, I was hooked on history as told by the people who experienced it. Not a textbook, but an emotional, real connection to an event or events in history.

Over the years, my Dad continued to add to his collection of war-related materials to one day turn into a book. With every attendance at a US LST Association Annual Convention, at every new book that came out explaining events of WWII in a new way, and every newspaper or magazine article that related in any way to his experience aboard the USS *LST-388* during WWII, the collection expanded. It became a never-ending project.

Never-ending, that is, until now.

In early 2016, at the age of 96, he began to ease off reading books about the war. This is when he turned it all, his entire collection, over to me to continue, and to turn into this book you now hold in your hands.

Combing through that collection, through the various versions of compiled journal entries, letters, articles, notes, photos, and postcards, I strived to compile it all into a book he could be proud of. I located and read all the references he mentioned, from Dwight D. Eisenhower's *Crusade in Europe*, to naval historian Samuel L. Morison's volumes on the war in North Africa, Sicily, and Salerno,

PREFACE

as well as France and Germany, to a 1944 issue of *Popular Science* Magazine. In addition, I read through months and months of Deck Logs for the USS *LST-388*, obtained from the National Archives in College Park, Maryland, in order to confirm dates and entries, and to fill in any existing gaps in the writings.

Sadly, my Dad would not live to see this final version of his journals and collected documents, articles, and photos. He passed away on December 3, 2016 at his home in Hayesville, North Carolina. Just the previous week I had been by his side, lost in his enormous smile. I knew then that he would not see this final version of his book. Honoring my promise to him, I have continued, and finally completed his book.

I, along with my Dad, want to share what we all now know as history, on a more personal level. May this book inspire you to share your own story, your own experience of history. It really does matter.

Barbara von der Osten
June 18, 2017 (Father's Day)

Acknowledgments

FIRST AND FOREMOST, this book would not be possible without the time and commitment of my father, during his three and half years serving in the United States Navy during World War II, and his continuous research throughout the post-war years.

Tremendous thanks go out to former USS *LST-388* shipmates Paul J. Roberts, Glenn Roberts, Al Mittlemeyer, Roger A. Goddard, Stewart Estes Wood, James Rodriques, and Bill Schellhorn (including Bill's daughter, Theresa Baciarini) for sharing their memories and photos with my father on many occasions.

There are several people who assisted with the research and editing of this final version of the book. To John Northrup, Ph.D. candidate in history at the University of South Florida, who read the initial manuscript and provided feedback on its historical content, while also offering suggestions, I owe monumental thanks. To Patricia Charpentier of *Writing Your Life*, who made me aware of potential improvements in my writing, and who provided initial edits and advice, I humbly thank you.

Thanks also goes out to Tammie Sewell of the Pinellas County Library in Largo, Florida for her dedication and determination to track down articles referenced in my father's original writings and notes. Tammie, you will never know how much your dedication to research, and your kindness, is appreciated. I am also grateful to Kari Williams, Senior Writer for the *Veterans of Foreign Wars* (VFW) magazine, and Zach Morris, editor of the *LST Scuttlebutt*, the official newsletter of the United States LST Association, for quickly locating articles mentioned in my father's notes.

There are always those who know you best, and who are willing to step away while you work on something you love. To my Army guy, Kevin Cantrell, who constantly listened to my tales about the role of

ACKNOWLEDGMENTS

the Navy during WWII, thank you for your love and patience. Most importantly, though, thank you for reminding me that this is a story about what happens between invasions, during the waiting, as much as it is about the invasions themselves.

And, last but by no means least, heartfelt thanks go to my Mom, Earlene Jackson von der Osten, who believed in this book from the beginning, encouraging first my Dad, and then me, to continue on to publication. We did it, Mom. We finally did it.

Foreword

WHILE IN THE UNITED STATES NAVY during World War II, 1942–1945, I kept a journal for a short while and numerous notes. As it turned out, I served most of my hitch on the USS *LST-388*.

After seventy years, I finally put this collected material in order. It is not only a sailor's story, but the history of a great landing ship and her dedicated crew.

Perhaps, one day, my grandchildren will be curious as to what little part their grandpa played in World War II and just might enjoy reading this book.

Robert W. von der Osten

Author's Note

THIS BOOK is a work of nonfiction. I have mentioned people and events as I remember them, and as recorded in my journals and notes during World War II.

I recognize that my memories of the events described in this book may differ from many other individuals and in no way do I discount their memories.

To the best of my recollection, the historical dates and events I include here are correct. Any missteps in stating historical facts are unintentional.

I am a history buff, and as such, I am aware that readers may not be familiar with many historical references I mention in this memoir. Rather than add lengthy descriptions, which might bog down the story I am trying to tell, I hope to spark the readers' curiosity enough to initiate their own research into our country's fascinating history.

Introduction

ON SEPTEMBER 1, 1939, Adolph Hitler's Nazi armies invaded Poland. I was nineteen years of age and out of high school a year. Through a friend of my father's, I was lucky to obtain a job making $16 per week as an office boy for Standard Oil Company of New Jersey. I worked in their Marine Department, located at 30 Rockefeller Plaza, Radio City, New York. People went about their lives, and no one seemed to believe a second world war had started.

I worked hard all day and attended New York University several nights a week at the Washington Square Branch. College was a terrible struggle. I had a long distance to travel from Staten Island to Radio City—first by bus, then ferry, and finally the subway—all of which took an hour and forty-five minutes. I would get so tired and have to push myself to study. School was not a fun thing and my grades were rather poor.

In spite of staying so busy, I did manage to read the *New York Times* every day while going to and from work and school. The events in Europe made interesting newspaper stories, but those events all seemed so far away. *Could a war really be going on?*

My grandparents were born in Germany, and my grandfather, William von der Osten, helped found St. John's Lutheran Church in Port Richmond, Staten Island, which offered a German-language service. Most of our social life revolved around St. Johns or its members.

Even though my father, Edwin von der Osten, had served in the US Navy during World War I, he remained extremely proud of his German heritage. I am too. My parents and grandparents could not have been better Christians or Americans.

When Hitler succeeded in one conquest after another, marching across Europe, everyone I knew tried to rationalize and justify his actions. These conflicts seemed so far away. We felt sure the American people would not allow the politicians to draw us into another European conflict. Even aviator Charles Lindberg worked towards keeping us out. Why become embroiled in another European mess?

In my grammar school, PS 19, I had a friend named Herman Kempf, who also attended St. John's Lutheran Church. He came to the United States from Germany in the early 1930s after Congress ratified the Twenty-First Amendment, ending Prohibition. His parents spoke little English, but his father found work at Rubsam & Horrmann Brewing Company in Stapleton, Staten Island. After graduating from high school, we often saw each other on weekends.

Herman followed Hitler's movements religiously. Although he thought Hitler was the greatest, I had some reservations. Hitler seemed too fanatical in the way he screamed and yelled and waved his arms, and I never understood a word he said. His funny mustache and hair style also looked odd to me.

One Sunday, Herman asked me to go to a German-American picnic on Staten Island. It turned out to be a German-American Bund, also known as the American Nazi Party, affair with perhaps 300 people in attendance. Most of them spoke German, which I did not understand. I found it strange to fly all those Nazi flags alongside the American flag. Many men wore Nazi-like uniforms, and I often heard people saying, "Heil, Hitler." The Führer's picture was everywhere.

German music played all afternoon, and when they launched into the German National Anthem, people stood and gave the straight-armed Nazi salute. In between songs, various people presented speeches, with the keynote talk given by the head of the German-American Bund, Fritz Kuhn. All the people and their words and actions felt so foreign and strange to me. I never went to another meeting.

In September 1939, when England and France declared war on Germany, we all felt it wasn't real. Surely, these countries would come together and settle their differences. Their lack of action

INTRODUCTION

during the first few months after the declaration appeared to support this notion.

Meanwhile, as the Spanish Civil War wound down, Fascist General Francisco Franco, with the aid of German and Italian soldiers and equipment, captured Madrid. We somewhat backed Franco because he stood against the communists. Germany and Italy used this Spanish Civil War as a testing ground for their men and equipment, but Spain didn't interest them too much. Some Americans felt concerned enough, however, to form the Abraham Lincoln Brigade, a group of individuals willing to travel to Spain to fight the Fascists.

Japan had invaded China in the early 1930s and acted on their cause of never-ending expansion. I collected pictures of this conflict and put them in a scrapbook. The Japanese equipment looked so awkward and old-fashioned, but they were ruthless in their treatment of their captives, killing thousands of Chinese people. This war took place far across the Pacific, and again, I believe, most Americans felt little concern for what was happening across the sea.

In November 1939, the Soviets invaded the small country of Finland, and most people in our community rooted for Finland. This little, underdog country held big Russia at bay for months. The press consistently portrayed Joseph Stalin, leader of the Soviet Union, as a mean Communist son-of-a-bitch, killing off thousands of his citizens who opposed him. Anti-communist feelings swept across the United States.

I knew only one Communist in my life—Bill Holska, a good friend of mine in grammar and high school. I think the Depression made him bitter and pushed him toward Communism. One day while on my way to work, I met him on the Staten Island Ferry. He talked about the coming revolution of workers of the United States and his belief that a Communist U.S. Government would bring prosperity to us all. A year later, I read in the *Staten Island Advance* newspaper that Bill committed suicide. What a tragedy! I thought a lot of him. If there was a Communist party on Staten Island, people kept it undercover.

We heard of the Nazi's mistreatment of the Jewish people. The American churches, both Protestant and Catholic, should have done more to condemn the concentration camps. Perhaps they didn't believe what was going on there. They did, however, protest the mistreatment of citizens in Russia. If we had concentrated on helping our allies in the West and let Russia hang a bit, perhaps the Communists would have failed, and the Soviet threat would not have been present. To my way of thinking, Stalin was as bad as Hitler. Why should we help him?

Most Staten Islanders I knew watched these confrontations around the world with indifference. The big interest of the year centered on the 1939 New York World's Fair. The fair focused on the world of tomorrow with a futuristic car by General Motors, television, color photography, nylon, air conditioning, cellophane, fluorescent lamps, the View-Master, and an early version of Smell-O-Vision, a system which released related scents at appropriate times throughout a movie. Americans' interest rested on the future, not the current state of affairs in far-off countries.

The war at sea was of great concern to my employer, Standard Oil Company of New Jersey, however, for it operated the largest tanker fleet in the world, many of which flew the Panamanian flag. A Standard Oil subsidiary, Panama Transport Company, owned many tankers manned by crews from different countries, including Germany. In 1939, the company replaced all German crews with seamen from other countries.

During this time, our office moved to Bayonne, New Jersey, so I was able to see many of these ships first hand.

The Germans crossed the Netherlands and Belgium borders on May 10, 1940. Fourteen days later the tanker, *Joseph Seep*, of the Panama Transport Company, manned by a Canadian crew, struck a mine dropped by a German plane in the roadstead, a sheltered area just off the coast, at Le Havre, France. She sank, a total loss. The war appeared more real to us now, although still so far away.

Many tankers flying the US flag, such as the *R.G. Stewart*, rescued survivors of allied ships torpedoed by German submarines. At first,

INTRODUCTION

German skippers aided the survivors of these downed ships. When the Germans torpedoed the tanker *Inverlifly*, they arranged for the transfer of survivors to the *R.G. Stewart*. They even gave the British captain a life jacket when they saw he had none.

Our office dealt only with American crews, but Warner Melvin's office worked with the Panama Transport Company. Their activities were always rather *hush-hush*.

Working during the day, going to college at night, and all the commuting required finally got to me in 1940. I decided to take time to enjoy life. I bought a car, took up skiing and bowling. I broke my kneecap trying to ski jump. My friend, Ed Abildness, and I decided to take up golf. If I broke a hundred, it was an accident. Ed belonged to Zion Lutheran Church, Port Richmond, Staten Island, and we spent a lot of time at his church as they had an active young people's group.

At my church, St. John's Lutheran, I joined the choir. Most welcomed me, but some members from the old-time families acted rather clannish. I liked one girl in the choir—Marge Ferenczi—and dated her from time to time.

Many of us felt the war in Europe would soon be over. France had surrendered, and England didn't seem to have much left to fight with.

In March 1941, an increase of more than 100% in pilot training by the Civilian Aeronautics Authority (CAA) was ordered as part of a program to expand the US Army Air Force. The CAA was authorized to train 45,000 students annually as pilots and required each to pass the ground school course before starting flight training.

During the summer of 1941, a friend, Warren Jensen, persuaded me to take the course at Wagner College on Staten Island. I received a certificate on August 26, 1941, stating I had passed the written exam necessary for a private pilot's license.

Now, I needed to pass a physical before the government would send me away for flight training. I saw a doctor in Stapleton, Staten Island, and everything went okay until he sat me down with two long strings in each hand. The strings were attached to movable pegs about fifteen feet away, and I needed to pull the strings and line up the pegs with each other.

Next, the doctor placed one end of a ruler, on top of which sat a needle-like stem holding a white bead, to the tip of my nose. As the bead moved back and forth, I was supposed to follow it with both of my eyes. Much to my dismay, I couldn't. I learned, for the first time, that I could not cross my eyes. The doctor said he could not pass me as I might land a plane ten feet off the ground. I felt bad about this. Warren, in the meantime, went on to get his wings.

Six weeks before the bombing of Pearl Harbor by the Japanese on December 7, 1941, I was called before the local draft board and, much to my surprise, classified 4-F, medically unfit for the draft. The report stated I had high blood pressure and a slight heart murmur. I've always wondered if I received that classification because my family physician, Dr. Pettit, was a personal friend of my Aunt Louise or because he liked the way I cut his grass. I felt and looked fine. I was embarrassed to be classified 4-F.

Pearl Harbor

Sunday, December 7, 1941. My friend, Ed Abildness, stopped by in his father's 1939 Dodge, and we decided to call on a girl we knew from church, Millie Peterson. It turned out we both got a date and the four of us decided to ride out to Al Deppe's on Richmond Avenue for an ice cream or hot dog.

The car radio blared with the music of the day as we talked and laughed, having a jolly time. All of a sudden, the music stopped for a special news bulletin. The Japanese had just bombed Pearl Harbor. The conflict was no longer *over there,* in distant countries. The United States was at war. The military immediately called all servicemen on leave back to duty. Our lives would soon change forever.

That evening as I drove along Richmond Terrace, I saw anti-aircraft guns on the roofs of old houses near the West Brighton shipyards. The government ordered blackouts, no visible lights after dark. I wondered if our country would also declare war on Germany

INTRODUCTION

as she was a partner of Japan. Could we possibly see fit to aid communist Russia?

Congress met on December 8, 1941, and declared war on both Japan and Germany. The American First Committee, an organization founded in opposition to the US entering World War II, offered no opposition.

Lindberg, one of my heroes, sought to aid his country in every way he could. President Franklin D. Roosevelt elected *not* to put him on active duty, although he was a colonel in the reserves, which I found unfair. I never cared for FDR or his children. His wife Eleanor was a wonderful woman but as ugly as the back fence.

The bombing of Pearl Harbor created great anxiety in people living along the West Coast of the United States. They feared the Japanese might attempt a landing in California once Japan realized the extent of the damage done to our Pacific fleet at Pearl Harbor.

All Japanese-Americans on the West Coast were suspected, without a shred of evidence, of belonging to a fifth column, intending to rise against the United States once the Japanese landed. President Roosevelt ordered all Japanese-Americans, although US citizens, interned and sent to camps on Native American reservations. These citizens—some second and third generation Americans—were removed from their homes with little notice, no time to dispose of or arrange for care of their property.

The United States press did not inform the public of this action. Placing these American citizens in concentration camps without any evidence of wrongdoing will be a black mark on our democracy for years to come. In the end, no Japanese-American was proved to be disloyal. Many young Japanese-Americans even joined the United States armed forces and fought in the war with distinction.

I did not realize what had been done to these poor people until years after the war. In college, the professor assigned a book written by a Japanese-American internee. The author described the treatment and hardships suffered by his people. This book disturbed me.

On the night of January 17–18, 1942, Germany torpedoed a Standard Oil Company tanker, *Allan Jackson*, flying the United States flag, off the North Carolina coast. Out of a crew of thirty-five, twenty-two lost their lives.

U-Boat Paradise

For six or seven months in 1942, German submarines, called U-boats, wreaked havoc in American waters. At first, they successfully attacked coastal shipping between Newfoundland and New York, torpedoing England-bound convoys near assembly ports.

Soon the attacks spread down to the coast of Florida, which prompted Winston Churchill to call the US East Coast a *U-Boat Paradise*.[1]

This stretch of ocean teemed with defenseless American and Allied shipping vessels as tanker fleets moved along this route from the oil ports of Venezuela. Protection provided by the US Navy was, for several months, completely inadequate.

It still surprises me that World War II had been going on for two full years before the US entered. Our country aided England with everything short of war, and yet the United States Navy had no plans for coastal convoys or multiplying small craft for escort duty.

In little over two months, January 1 to March 12, 1942, German U-boats sunk or damaged approximately sixty tankers, and most took place within 300 miles of the US coast, between Charleston and New York.

Many of my Standard Oil Company co-workers knew the men killed or injured in these incidents because they signed them on before voyages. The paymaster responsible for paying the crews also worked out of our office. All the ships torpedoed up and down the eastern seaboard caused our staff much concern.

PART I
I JOIN THE NAVY

Left: Pamphlet I received from the U.S. Navy Recruiting Station: *Instructions For Men Who Wish To Be Enlisted In The Navy.*

Below: Oath recited by me on February 12, 1942 as I was sworn in to the US Navy.

U. S. NAVY RECRUITING STATION

INSTRUCTIONS FOR MEN WHO WISH TO BE ENLISTED IN THE NAVY

After you have passed the Doctor's examination and are ready to be enlisted, you will have to sign the following certificate:

"I have had this contract fully explained to me; I understand it; and certify that no promise of any kind has been made to me concerning assignment to duty, or promotion during my enlistment."

A great many men sign this certificate without understanding fully what it means. Some men sign it without knowing what the Shipping Articles are.

The **Shipping Articles** are the articles or conditions under which you come into the Naval Service. You bind yourself to do certain things and the United States Government binds itself to give you certain things in return for your services. What do you agree to do? What does the Government agree to do? Until you can answer these questions fully, you must not sign the articles. You must always find out exactly what they mean by asking one of the men in the office.

Read the **Shipping Articles** carefully. Take the first one. According to this article, you agree:

To enter the service of the United States;
To go where you are ordered to go, on any ship or any station that the Government sees fit to send you, but the Government does not agree to send you to any particular ship or station.

U. S. NAVY RECRUITING STATION

This Must be Read Carefully by All Applicants Who Have Been Accepted, Before They Are Sworn In

OATH OF ALLEGIANCE

I do solemnly swear that I will bear true faith and allegiance to the UNITED STATES OF AMERICA and that I will serve them honestly and faithfully against all their enemies whomsoever and that I will obey orders of the President of the UNITED STATES, and the orders of the officers appointed over me, according to the Rules and Articles for the Government of the Navy. And I do further swear or affirm that all statements made by me as now given in this record are correct.

Before you can be enlisted in the Navy, you must take this oath which you have just read. When you have taken this oath, you become one of the regular men of the Navy; and, like all the other men of the Navy, you must obey the regulations of the Navy and the orders of the officers and petty officers of the Navy.

Probably, this is the first time in your life you have ever taken an oath. Do you know just what an oath means — what is it? An oath is a solemn promise made by one person to another person. In Christian countries, an oath is usually made in the name of GOD, or in the name of what is held most sacred by the person who makes the oath. When you take the oath of allegiance, you make a solemn promise to the Recruiting Officer. The Recruiting Officer is the agent of the United States. Therefore, you make a promise to the United States of America.

It is a very solemn and binding promise; and you should not make this promise unless you know exactly what you promise to do, and unless you have made up your mind to carry out your promise to the best of your ability and conscience.

Read the oath carefully. First, you swear that you will bear true FAITH and ALLEGIANCE to the United States of America. What does that mean? What is FAITH? What is ALLEGIANCE?

I Join the Navy

PATRIOTIC SPIRIT ran high once the United States entered the war. Both the Army and Navy had more applicants than they could handle. I felt uncomfortable with my draft classification of 4-F, medically unfit for the draft. I wanted to do my bit.

On January 29, 1942, just after my twenty-second birthday, I took the bull by the horns. My work at the office did not feel like enough to help the war effort. Plus, it was boring. Without talking to anyone about it, I went to 90 Church Street in Manhattan and applied to join the United States Navy and was accepted with no problems. They sent me home to await a date for swearing in and notified my draft board #293.

A few days after I joined the Navy, February 2, 1942, the Standard Oil tanker *W.L. Steed* was torpedoed by a German U-boat, then sunk by shell fire off the Delaware coast. The entire crew escaped the sinking ship in open lifeboats but were exposed to heavy snowfall, tossed by the waves, and lashed by icy winds of a winter storm. They perished one by one. Out of a crew of thirty-eight, only four ultimately survived. Again, the office buzzed with activity.

Staten Islanders knew many of these Standard Oil Company tankers. They were accustomed to seeing the ships undergoing repairs at the Bethlehem Shipyard and many of the families of the seamen who crewed the tankers lived on Staten Island.

I was officially accepted into the United States Navy February 12, 1942, Abraham Lincoln's birthday, and sworn in by an old submarine commander at 90 Church Street, Manhattan. Once again, the Navy sent me home to await the call into active duty. There was no room for me in boot camp at that time.

On February 27, 1942, the Esso tanker *R.P. Resor* was torpedoed off Barnegat Light at the entrance to New York Harbor where she remained afloat for two days. Crowds along the New Jersey shore witnessed the huge pall of black smoke of the sinking ship. All but two of the ship's complement were lost. This action brought the war very close to home.

What follows are journal entries made as I experienced boot camp, training, ship time, liberty, and war. The dated text represents actual entries made on the dates listed, and then supplemented with information I have gleaned over the years about those events and times. Also included are details of my time away from the base or ship. Liberty (granted time off) was an extremely important part of my life, and, from what I could tell, was so for all sailors and soldiers. Reading, playing cards, and granted time off (liberty) served as distractions from the intensity of war and provided a boost to morale. I took advantage of every liberty granted during the war, and made the best of them I could.

Boot Camp
Newport, Rhode Island

BOOT CAMP proved to be an intensive experience. A combination of physical training, exercises in the field, and indoor classes whipped us all in to shape quickly. I ran track in high school and was a good swimmer prior to joining the Navy, so I didn't find it too difficult most of the time. Yet, it was extremely different from my life up until this point. It all started with a crowd of new recruits gathered in Manhattan.

March 17, 1942—Today, St. Patrick's Day, I reported to 90 Church Street for active duty. After a medical and lunch in a drugstore, we marched to the Colonial Line Pier and boarded the old riverboat, USS *Commet*. She sailed for Providence, Rhode Island, at 11:00 p.m. in the rain. My roommate was a comical fellow from Manhattan named Tom Walsh. Most of the recruits hung out at the bar all evening. The whistle blew constantly in the dense fog. I didn't get much sleep during my first night in the navy.

March 18, 1942—The USS *Commet* was fogbound for hours, so we didn't get to Providence until late. Once there, I took a bus to Newport. First they gave me a terrific medical and haircut. Hundreds of us went down a big open barracks stark naked. Every few feet, someone checked us for some physical or medical defect. If we were okay, they put a certain mercurochrome mark on our backs. At the end, if we had a specific design painted on us, we passed the medical.

I am a collector of postcards, and found them a good way to document my travels and experiences during the war. Here is one of them that shows the training barracks at our boot camp in Newport, Rhode Island.

I was okay. The doctor noted my blood pressure but let me by. In the process we were also sheared of most of our hair. I was then issued, along an assembly line, navy clothes that almost fit. My civilian clothes will be sent home. I carried my gear to the barracks and fell asleep immediately. At least I look like a sailor now.

March 19, 1942—Today, I started the tedious job of stenciling my clothes. What a large camp this is. I am in Barracks D, Company 407, in an annex with eight other fellows.

My basic training at this big camp in Newport, Rhode Island lasted from March 18 to May 8, 1942. I drilled and learned the basic facts needed to become a sailor and was kept so busy that I did not have time to keep a daily journal.

The camp was a beautiful place, a permanent base. Our barracks were frame, but many were brick. There was a long sloping parade ground, and at the foot of the parade ground, was a pier, where the USS *Constellation*, sister ship of the USS *Constitution*, was moored.

BOOT CAMP

On the Homefront, my mother, Henrietta, served as Chairman of the St. John's Lutheran Church Unit of the Port Richmond Branch of the Red Cross in Staten Island, NY. My father, Edwin, worked as a checker on the New York waterfront, helping to get ships loaded for the war effort.

Visits from family and friends were always welcome while in boot camp. My best friend from Staten Island, Ed Abildness, who joined the Navy the day after me, and his sister Ester are on the left. My sister, Ruth, and I are on the right.

Highlights of my time here included winning the freestyle swimming race. (I believe it was 220 yards.) We swam against all the other companies in the camp.

Liberty [time off] was given only on Sunday afternoons. My mother and father, other relatives, and friends often visited me on my liberties, and we spent time in the city of Newport, Rhode Island.

Hardships at the camp were eased by my best friend, Ed Abildness, who joined the day after me, being in the next barracks. We often got together in the evenings. Ed and I took several tests designed to show what we were capable of doing for the navy. We both stated radioman, among other things, that we wanted to do.

Group of sailors in boot camp, including Ed Abildness (far left) and myself (in the middle).

As time went on, Ed and I learned a few tricks. Several afternoons toward the end of our training, we turned left at the same time the company turned right, and we skipped drill. Drilling with heavy rifles almost killed us. We went down to the bay and sat by the shore until the drill was over.

Ed was sent to the RCA radio school in New York the day before I left Newport, and that was the last Ed and I saw of each other until after the war.

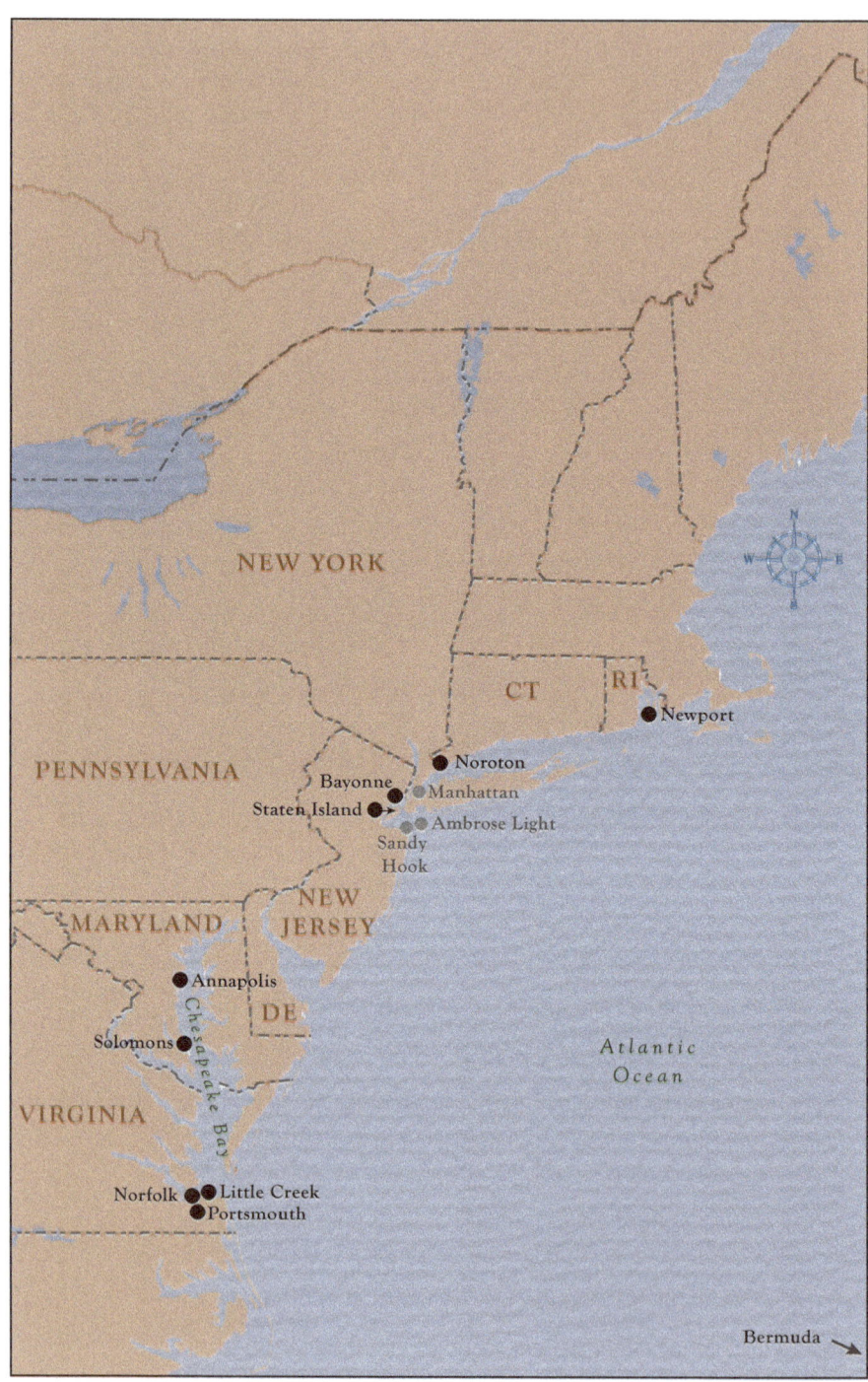

U.S. Naval Radio Training School
Noroton, Connecticut

I HAD MADE IT THROUGH boot camp and was next sent to the U.S. Naval Radio Training School in Noroton, Connecticut. This four-month program focused on communications, including radio operations, International Morse Code, blinker code, and the use of signal flags.

May 8, 1942—Today, I left Newport, Rhode Island for the USN Radio School at Noroton, Connecticut. Our group left Newport by special train at 9:00 A.M. and arrived at 4:00 P.M. This is a beautiful school. It is situated in a quiet community just above Stamford, and before the war, it was an old soldiers' home. The vine covered buildings are arranged around a park-like campus. There are about 700 men in this school. I was given a physical checkup and then assigned to my new quarters. I am in Company 7 in Barracks E and feel very strange here this first day.

May 9, 1942—Although I tried to get liberty this weekend (Sunday is Mother's Day), I had no luck. This place is so free and different from boot camp. I understand it is quite a hard course that is given here. Called home and expect to see Mom, my sister Ruth, and friend Marge tomorrow. Had to wash my bag and hammock. The ship's service is in a little red barn. The company commander is quite a character. He treats us like his children. The food is good and served by mess cooks. If you happen to be at the front of the table you get the best, but if you are at the far end you have to fight for the meat sometimes. Bert Thomas sleeps on the bunk under me, and John Sheridan, a Staten Island boy, sleeps in the bunk next to mine.

May 10, 1942—Went to church in the little chapel they have here. In the afternoon, Mom, Dad, Ruth, and Marge came to see me. I was able to take them through the school and grounds. Bert Thomas seems to like my sister Ruth very much and intends to write her. I think he likes all girls for a time until he sees another.

May 11, 1942—Each company has about 60 men in it. A petty officer is in charge. A tough 1/C bos'n mate, who we call Windy, has us in tow. He is only about 5'6" tall. He swears at us continuously in his deep voice but we know he really doesn't mean it. He is really swell to the fellows.

Every day at radio school was more or less the same. We woke up early and went to colors at 0800, an inspiring ceremony held in the center of the campus near the huge flagpole. After the flag raising, some of [world heavyweight champion boxer (1926–1928)] Gene Tunney's specialists led the entire student body in exercises.

School wasn't too hard for me except for the [Morse] code. I struggled with the code for weeks, and then all of a sudden, it came to me. I rose to the top of the class. (When I graduated I had a 3.93 average, a score topped by only one man in the class.)

During my stay at this school, I spent one week as mess cook. I waited on two tables of chowhounds who never stopped yelling for their food. The fellows at the one end grabbed everything, and the ones on the other end had to wait. Afterwards, we had to wash all the dishes. Then our tables had to be scoured and the floor swabbed. Once we finished cleaning, we worked in the spud locker shelling peas, washing spinach, taking eyes out of potatoes, and cleaning melons.

I spent another week as escort in the duty office where I escorted trucks and visitors through the grounds. It rained constantly that week.

Our company included a nice bunch of fellows except for a few wise guys who liked to keep everyone awake. These creeps talked of nothing but sex, bragging about how manly they were. Some claimed they had relations with a couple of Noroton girls, while on guard duty, through the wire fence. Believe this, and I'll tell you another.

George Sindt from Woodhaven, Long Island, was my best friend at radio school. He formerly worked in a pork store. Bill Salitsky, a Russian who played football for Miami and was married, worried a lot about school.

The USO provided good entertainment for us. We saw the blind pianist Alec Templeton; actress Tallulah Bankhead; various composers such as the man who wrote "Melancholy Baby," the National Barn Dance, a country music variety show; and Carl Hoff and his orchestra. I enjoyed watching the movie, *New Wine*, the story of Franz Schubert.

Sometimes, fellows from the school entertained us as well.

The special train that took us to New York City on weekends was an experience. On the way to the city, our sailors were lucky to have a seat, and coming back to school, all hell broke loose as at least half the sailors were under the influence. Those who didn't go home had wild times in New York and bragged about making out with girls.

On one trip, the train broke down in a tunnel departing Grand Central Terminal. It was one of the hottest days of the summer, and we all were worn out from the heat. My uniform was stained red in the back from the train seats.

> *August 21, 1942*—We had our code, typing, materials, and procedure tests today. I passed all tests and am rated at 33 words per minute in code and 57 words per minute typing.
>
> *August 26, 1942*—I was made Radioman 3/C today. My average tied for second highest in the class. Graduation was an impressive outdoor ceremony before the entire school. Mom sold my 1940 Chevrolet for $525. Fourteen months ago, I paid $730 for it.
>
> *August 27, 1942*—I learned today that I am headed for Norfolk and the amphibious force. No one seems to know just what the amphibious force is.

Amphibious Force Training Base
Joint Communication School
Little Creek, Virginia

EARLY DURING THE WAR, military planners realized there was a need to land tanks and troops directly on hostile foreign shores. This required a new form of training.

Carved out of farmlands and swamps, the Amphibious Force Training Base at Little Creek, Virginia was in its early stages of development when I arrived in 1942. I was to attend the Joint Communication School, which meant both Navy sailors and Army soldiers trained together in communications. Up to this point, the Army and Navy had had independent communication systems, but for an amphibious operation, these systems needed to be coordinated. We all had our work cut out for us in the days ahead.

September 2, 1942—We arrived at Cape Charles, Delaware, at 6:00 A.M., and immediately boarded the oldest of the Cape Charles-Norfolk ferries. The boat was very crowded because of the large number of boots [apprentice seamen] on board who were going to the battleship USS *Alabama*. They fed us in the very bottom of the ship in a crude dining room. The fellow that served the lousy food had the nerve to demand a tip. The ferry took three hours to cross to Norfolk.

We hung around downtown Norfolk for three hours before being taken to the receiving station. It was so hot and desolate that it had to be a duplicate of a desert camp. After lousy chow, they jammed us into a truck and sent us to the main operating base. About 3,000 men slept in a big mess hall or drill hall. The bunks were very close together. I slept on a cot without blankets or mattress. It felt like I was sleeping in a den of thieves. At night we had liberty and went on a trolley to Norfolk to see the movie *Kings Row*. On the way, a cop got on the trolley and threw a black man off the car because he wasn't sitting far enough to the rear. I didn't get much sleep.

September 3, 1942—This morning, we got up at 6:00 A.M. After much hanging around, we were jammed in a bus that was used for sightseeing in the recent New York World's Fair. We rode for about 15 miles to the dustiest, desolate place on earth, Little Creek. This is our home for the next four weeks.

We stand in line for an hour for chow, eat in ten minutes, and then stand in line in order to wash our cups and plates. The metal cups and plates are army issue. There are no shows or entertainment of any kind. The place is miles from any town.

I am told that three weeks ago, there were only three buildings, and now there are about 30 buildings. The carpenters are still putting the roof on our barracks. No roads or sidewalks, just dust and mud. I have been made petty officer of the Noroton boys. There are soldiers here living in other barracks and going through the same routine as we are. It is more like the army than the navy. No drinking water for six blocks from any barracks. Our address is Amphibious Force Training Base, Joint Communication School.

September 4, 1942—Another day in this place God forgot. Fellows just walk in and out of here. Liberty or not, the guard doesn't ask questions. Fellows come in three hours late, and nothing is said. We have been here two days, and out of 64 men, in my barracks, ten have gone over the hill (left base without granted leave). I have done nothing all day except sleep, sweat, and swat pesky flies. I am disgusted with this place, especially with the sanitary conditions. If I get out of here without getting some disease, I will be lucky.

There doesn't seem to be anyone directly in charge of us. A chief walked in and shifted the bunks and then disappeared. An ensign walked in and ordered us to clean up the head—nothing done. They fixed the boilers and, in turning on the water, somehow the toilet bowls started to overflow with the excrement in them. Thousands of flies collect there. The mess hall equipment is filthy. Piles of discarded food can be found all over the floor.

September 5, 1942—Things seem to be a little more organized than yesterday. We had a muster and found that eight Noroton boys out of the 20 who came here have gone over the hill. In a day and a half, they have paved many of the roads. It isn't so hot today, making the place a little more bearable. School starts Monday.

September 6, 1942—Today, I was not ashamed to admit that I was very lonely. In the afternoon, Davis and I hitched a ride to Norfolk and saw a show. Davis wanted to see another show, so I left him and wandered around Norfolk. Much to my surprise, I found the nicest USO. It was formerly a private home. They served supper and then had services. A Chaplin Stone spoke. He had a rank of commander. I hitched back about 9:30 p.m.

September 7, 1942—Showered all day, making this place one big mud pond. The chow is still lousy and tastes like aluminum. I just can't eat it. School started today. An ensign described beachhead landing operations. There are no seats, so we must lay on the floor and take code with a pencil. We had a semaphore class.

September 8, 1942—Went to school with no furniture or electricity but plenty of dirt. Had lectures in semaphore, camouflage, and had some code. I also laid on the floor and slept. Boy, is it hot! Chow line seems to be getting longer. Went to Norfolk with Bob Randolph from Staten Island. I would like to go to the burlesque but do not have the nerve to buy a ticket.

September 9, 1942—Chow line is getting longer and longer. A Major Clark had a lecture on aircraft identification. They took all of us, including the army fellows, and had us do sit-up exercises out in the hot sun. They say we are going to be placed in Navy-Army combat teams to hit the beach with the army and communicate with the landing craft.

September 10, 1942—What a chow line! Learned to operate a walkie-talkie. An army sergeant was the instructor. Had a lecture on camouflage. Will they ever get anything to drink except ice tea? There is a camouflaged airport across the street that looks like an ordinary field. There is one hand pump here for 2,000 men to get their water. In the afternoon it gets so hot, I can hardly think.

September 11, 1942—Believe it or not, we drank from new china cups and ate from new china bowls. Still the big chow line. Had a lecture on pyrotechnics [flares, rockets, etc.]. Practice in semaphore and blinker. Had a field day today and expect a captain's inspection. No mail since I arrived.

September 13, 1942—Sunday. Although I didn't have liberty, I went to Norfolk where I played records at the USO, swam at the Y.M.C.A., and ate a free supper at the USO. Back at camp at 11:00 p.m. I wonder if the Red Cross is a paper organization. Haven't seen anything run by them.

September 18, 1942—Had a bad headache today. It is hot, and chow is terrible. Admiral Hewitt and some general are going to inspect camp tomorrow. Letter from my twin brother Herb indicates he is trying to get into the service terribly hard.

September 19, 1942—Received leave from 3:00 p.m. today, Saturday, until 10:00 A.M. Monday. Randy and I ran like the devil and made the Cape Charles Ferry. Had to wait six hours for the New York Train. Discovered Randy's father was on the same ship with my father in World War I, the USS *Kroonland*.

September 20, 1942—Arrived home around 8:30 A.M. Sure appreciated Mom's cooking. Had a nice time with family and friends. I miss my car though. Left on the 11:15 train from Pennsylvania Station.

September 21, 1942—Arrived back at Little Creek at 9:30 A.M. Learned more on walkie-talkie and a set called TBY [a portable transmitter-receiver]. We started standing watches. Boy, am I tired!

September 22, 1942—In school, we had navigation chart reading, semaphore, procedure, and worked with TBYs. Chief gave me a letter stating that I am in the service so I can get a refund on my license plates. Rumor is that we are no longer going to be on combat teams but will go to 300-foot tank landing ships. Two 2nd class technicians left today, and it seems that they were never supposed to have been here. I am barracks captain again.

September 23, 1942—School as usual. Chow is a little better, but the utensils are as greasy as ever.

September 24, 1942—Today, I stood from 12:30 to 4:00 p.m. in the pay line. There was a near riot when some fellows tried to chisel in. After getting my $35, I went with a friend to Ocean View where we had a steak and some beer.

September 25, 1942—School, only new thing was army map reading. Went to Norfolk and saw the movie *Wake Island*. The barracks weren't swept at all today, and the place looks like a pig pen.

September 27, 1942—Sunday. Went to the beautiful First Lutheran Church on College Avenue, Norfolk. I met a very interesting fellow at the USO. He is from Alabama and graduated from Berry College. It is a college where 90% of the students work. Henry Ford is interested in it.

September 28, 1942—School. Six boys are being shipped out tomorrow. Took code in new code room. Read a good article in *Readers Digest* entitled "At Dawn, I Die."

September 30, 1942—Went to Norfolk to the Lutheran Service Center and read half the book *The Man Nobody Knows* by Bruce Barton. I have developed a bad dose of the hives.

October 2, 1942—The hives are driving me nuts. They gave me two shots and covered me with Calamine lotion. Got leave and took the next Cape Charles ferry. At New Castle, I hitched a ride on a trailer truck, which luckily brought me to Elizabeth traffic circle. A Coast Guardsman gave me a lift within a block of home. What luck!

October 3, 1942—The hives are terrible, but at least, I am home. Went to Dr. Petit and got a shot and some pills.

October 4, 1942—My father suggested I go to the Brooklyn Navy Base and try to get my leave extended because of the hives. I went but received little sympathy.

October 5, 1942—Back at base. Lectures in first aid, semaphore, etc. Received pay—$36. Tonight, Larry caught the fellow in the signal tower's attention a mile away. We talked by blinker for a while.

From what I could tell, most sailors did not like Norfolk, Virginia or many of its residents. It is said that many residents put signs out front saying "Dogs and Sailors keep off the grass." I never had any desire to go back to Norfolk when I returned to civilian life. One disgusted sailor (Letitia Lindsay) even wrote a poem entitled "Ode to Norfolk".

Ode to Norfolk

When the Lord was designing creation,
He laid out a smooth stretch of sand
Surrounded by watery inlets
That crept in to form a swamp land.

Thick forests of pine and of oak trees
Twined silent with creepers and berries
Formed home for the stealthy, strong red men
Who hunted and fished from their wherries.

AMPHIBIOUS FORCE TRAINING BASE

Then white men came valiantly sailing
And landed and planted a cross;
Pushed inland until they reached Jamestown;
Shot Indians to prove who was boss.

They scattered in every direction,
New towns rose on every smooth spot;
But the ones to settle Old Norfolk
Were the ones who should have been shot.

Time shifted the sand bar with sewage;
Scum slithered and slipped in from shore;
The Chesapeake strove to be cleansing
But only brought litter the more.

Tis here where they do all things backward,
Where dirt never drives between rains,
Where prices mount faster and faster
And money is better than brains.

It's full of an infernal odor
A famed international smell
Till the average American sailor
Would rather be anchored in Hell.

Yes, it's back to the West for yours truly
A sadder but much wiser chap
Still wondering why those first people
Ever put Norfolk town on the map.

U.S. Naval Amphibious Training Base
Solomons, Maryland

WITH OUR TRAINING at Little Creek complete, the Navy next shuttled us to the newly created U.S. Naval Amphibious Training Base in Solomons, Maryland, located on the Chesapeake Bay. Here we would be split up into crews, assigned to ships, and gain actual experience aboard ship.

October 13, 1942—We shipped out today on a little, ancient, excursion boat. Everyone had to wear life jackets the entire time. Our destination was to be Solomons, Maryland but something happened, and we ended up in the St. Helena Barracks in Portsmouth. The place is unbelievably small. Large lockers, Simmons mattresses, good chow, beautiful canteen, including beer, and a large gym. I played some basketball. We will be here for only a few days. Met some fellows from my old company in Newport. Five went to diesel school, and one is on a tin can (a Destroyer class ship).

October 16, 1942—Arose at 4:00 A.M. and boarded another tiny, excursion boat, the cattle boat *Lillian Ann*. Four hundred and thirty-five men jammed on this tub, which in peace time would be overcrowded with 75 on it. We were on the *Lillian Ann* for 15 hours. It rained most of the time as we sailed up the Chesapeake Bay to

Solomons. I sat on a camp stool all the way. We ate one sandwich in 15 hours. When we got to our destination, they told us to roll our trousers to our knees. Everyone carried a heavy sea bag, mattress, and hammock one-third of a mile through mud that was over our ankles. It splashed all over me from head to foot. At 9:00 p.m. it took me an hour to find my sea bag for no one carried his own from the ship. Someone had dropped mine in the mud. Our gang was well separated. I went to sleep disgusted and exhausted.

October 17, 1942—It is still raining. What a mess! Our barracks are full of mud, which must be cleaned out with brushes and brooms. I stood for an hour in the mud and rain for something to eat. There is a small store or canteen. No liberty is granted. They are breaking us up into crews.

October 18, 1942—Eric Walz and I went to church. We stood two hours in line for chow. Then I read the rest of the day as there was nothing else to do.

October 20, 1942—Took a two-hour hike with 100 others. We could not get out of line—no freedom. They marched us out of camp into the country and marched us right back. This must be like prison! I did receive six letters today.

October 23, 1942—I am completely disgusted with this place. The disorganization here is unbelievable! My *Readers Digest* was stolen from under my mattress. Two of the fellows are having a fist fight as I write this. I have never seen such low morale. It seems the commissioned officers do not know the least bit of what they are doing.

October 24, 1942—Played cards on this dreary day. I was moved to Barracks 14. Ninety percent of the fellows are Southerners. Eric Walz was called to crew 4008. It seems you just get a good friend and then they separate you. He is going to Newport News at 4:00 A.M. tomorrow.

October 28, 1942—Received a letter from brother Herb today. He said that Jack Horan, one of his best friends, received his ensign commission and thinks he will be assigned to the Amphibious Force. At night, I saw the movie, *Ten Gentlemen from West Point*. Also today, I was assigned as a 3rd Class Radio Operator to crew #4023. We will soon take over the USS *LST-388* now under construction.

In preparation for an eventual assault on the European mainland, the US Army focused on building field guns and tanks. But how were they to land these on the hostile enemy beaches across the sea? Unlike in WWI, deep-water harbors and ports would not be available for the Allies' use. Eventually it was determined that a new type of landing ship was needed, one that could land on a beach, or enter a shallow port.

By May of 1942, the building of these new landing ships, called LSTs, which stood for Landing Ship, Tank, had become the number one priority over all other types of ships. Shipbuilders all over the country were directed to focus on the building of LSTs, one of which was the USS *LST-388*.

October 29, 1942—Had school, blinker, semaphore, etc. I like the crew a lot. We saw the movie, *They Ride by Night*, in the new amphitheater.

October 31, 1942—I was on watch 1600 to 2000. We have been told that our crew will leave for Norfolk on Monday. There is a big sea battle going on in the Pacific near the Solomon Islands.

November 1, 1942—A United States aircraft carrier officially declared sunk. The British are on the offensive in Africa. Our crew moved to the second story of the barracks. Everyone was given a physical, and we have been told we will be leaving tomorrow morning. I found an old letter from Mom with two dollars in it.

November 2, 1942—Crew #4023 was put on board a small excursion tub, the *Lillian Ann*, for the trip to Paradise Creek near Norfolk. Upon arrival, we all thought this place was appropriately named for it sure was paradise compared to Solomons.

November 5, 1942—Today we were put aboard USS *LST-384* as a training crew. There were two training crews aboard. The ship's company were fellows who had left Solomons only two weeks earlier. Only a handful of the men had ever been on a seagoing ship before. It was amazing how fast various members of our gang caught on to the many ship operations and maneuvers. After seeing what jobs some of the others had aboard, I decided that being a radio operator wasn't so bad. Everyone seemed to pitch in and were eager to learn their duties.

November 6, 1942—The battleship, USS *Indiana*, pulled in and docked across from us. I saw Tom Walz from my old Newport Company coming down the USS *Indiana* gangplank. He is going to take us through her tomorrow. Many men from my old company are on her. He says there are about 2,800 men on the USS *Indiana*. There is a terrific battle going on in Africa.

November 7, 1942—Had fire drills all day. We were taken through the USS *Indiana*. What a ship! Walter Wanamaker is an Electrician 3/C. Rommel [senior German army officer] seems to be losing in Africa.

November 8, 1942—Several of us went to church on the battleship, USS *Wyoming*. It is an old but powerful battleship. As there was no Protestant chaplain, the service was conducted by a Catholic priest. We had fire and abandon ship drills all afternoon. I was assigned to #10 life raft, which is just aft [back] of the radio room. It will take us longer than most to get our raft over.

November 9, 1942—Lectures on collision duties and more drills.

November 10, 1942—The U.S. invaded North Africa. Some French are resisting the invasion and assisting the Germans. Many French warships have been either sunk by the British or scuttled [deliberately sunk] by their crews. Communiques say things are going well.

November 11, 1942—The *Esso Augusta*, a tanker, pulled in at the pier. I remember working on her crew problems for Standard Oil (my pre-war employer). After getting paid $71, I was able to send $100 home.

November 13, 1942—Sailed today and all hands had to stay topside until we passed outside the nets. Anchored off Little Creek. We will maneuver with other amphibious craft. The signalmen get my goat as they think they are so important. I can stand a signal watch, but not one of the signalmen can stand a radio watch.

November 16, 1942—Stood radio watches as we maneuvered the ship with the ships' company. This ships' company couldn't teach us much because they don't know much yet. The US fleet has won a great victory in the Pacific.

November 17, 1942—Left the USS *LST-384* by launch with our sea bags, etc. One of the fellows slipped, and his bag and hammock fell into the bay. It was dark when we arrived at Little Creek, where we were then taken by bus to Paradise Creek.

Now it was finally time to put all our training to work. It was time to get our own ship.

PART II
USS *LST-388*

The story of the USS LST-388 and her crew as I experienced it while serving as a radioman aboard her, and from information I collected in later years.

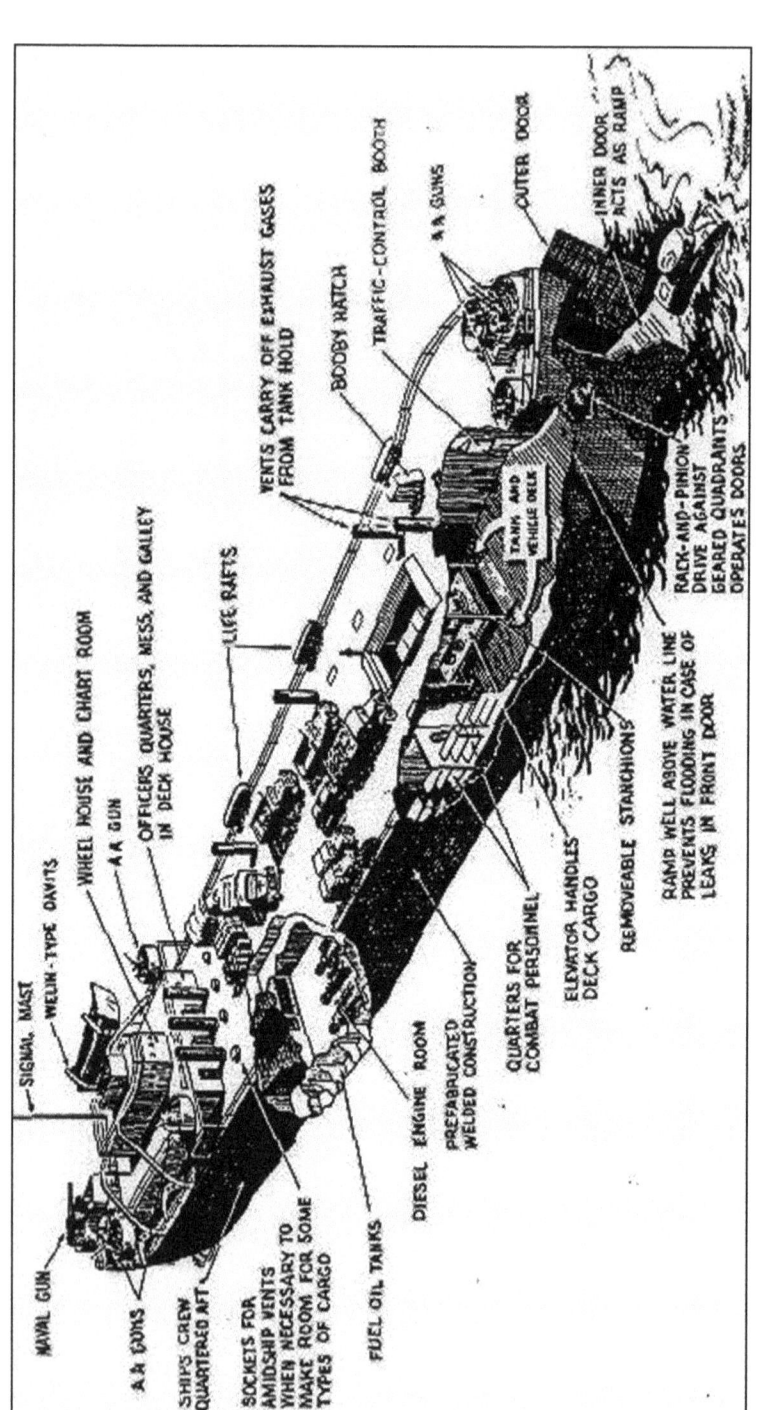

LANDING SHIP TANK (LST)

A Guide to Ship Acronyms Used in this Book

NAVY Amphibious Force LANDING CRAFT

"OCEANGOING VESSELS of over 200 feet in length overall, specifically designed for landing operations, fall within the category of Landing Ships. LS is used as a prefix in special designations of these types. The term landing craft is generally applied to non-oceangoing vessels of less than 150 feet in length overall designed for use in landing operations. The designation LC (Landing Craft) is therefore used, with appropriate modification to indicate particular types."

SOURCE: *Allied Landing Craft of World War II*, Navy Institute Press, Fourth Printing, 1989.

LST (Landing Ship, Tank). Amphibious assault ship for transporting vehicles, cargo, ammunition and troops to beaches. (328 ft, with a 50 ft. beam).

Once beached, ship bow doors open and a ramp is let down for offloading tanks and other vehicles.

LCT (Landing Craft, Tank). Amphibious assault craft for landing up to five 30-ton, four 40-ton, or three 50-ton tanks on beachheads via a bow ramp.

LST 388

At Sea: LST-388 transporting LCT-845 on the top deck (courtesy of Atlantic Fleet Sales, Warship Photo Graphs).

LCI (Landing Craft, Infantry). Amphibious assault craft used to land large numbers of infantry (troops) directly onto beaches. Troops disembark via deployable gangways rather than elaborate bow doors. Troop Capacity: 180–210 troops.

LCM (Landing Craft, Mechanized). Amphibious assault craft for transporting of vehicles, cargo and troops from ship to shore; for use in amphibious landing operations. Unloaded via bow ramp. Troop Capacity: 60–100

LCVP (Landing Craft, Vehicle, Personnel). Amphibious assault landing craft used to transport cargo, tracked and/or untracked vehicles, and troops from amphibious assault ships to beachheads or piers, unloading via bow ramp. Also known as Higgins Boats. Troop Capacity: 36

USS *LST-388*
NCZY (Call Letters)

With boot camp and training behind me, I was made RM/3 (Radioman Third Class) and assigned to Crew #4023. On November 20, 1942, our ship, the USS *LST-388* was commissioned and became my home for the next two years and nine months.

She didn't look like much. Some say she looked like a huge wooden shoe floating backward. Another described her as like a huge whale casting up all kinds of war material from her jaw-like bow. She didn't have a name, just a number, displayed in large white letters on her sides.

The USS *LST-388* was but one of more than a thousand ships of her class built in American shipyards over the course of the war. Originating from British specifications, these vessels were capable of transporting tanks across the Atlantic, from the United States to the beaches of Africa and Europe. They could also be modified to carry troops, vehicles of all kinds, and even trains.

One of the things that made them so unique was their ability to run right up on a beach at low tide, and retract at high tide. However, during the ship's planning stages, the question became one of how to design a ship with a deep draft for ocean travel, but shallow enough for beaching. The answer came in the form of a large ballast system which could be filled for ocean crossings, making the ship heavier, and then pumped out, making it lighter for beaching operations.

The final design of the LST distributed the weight of the ship over a greater area, which enabled her to ride higher in the water when set for beaching.

In both the United States and British Navies, these ships were more popularly known as *Large Slow Targets* rather than Landing Ship, Tanks. This is where their weakness lay. They had a top speed of nine knots, a hair more than ten miles per hour. For an amphibious (beaching) operation, they could carry up to twenty tanks on the main deck and several lighter vehicles, such as trucks and towed guns, on the weather deck. The early ships, like the USS *LST-388*, contained an elevator to the tank deck, but later ships had a ramp, which allowed faster unloading via the bow doors.

USS *LST-388*

Laid Down: June 20, 1942 at Newport News Shipbuilding & Drydock Co.
Launched: Sept. 28, 1942.
Sponsor: Barbara Ann Bessee
Length: 328 ft.
Beam: 50 ft.

November 20, 1942—The USS *LST-388* was commissioned today at NOB [Naval Operating Base], Norfolk, Virginia. A very short ceremony was held on the fantail. We were all in our dress blues.

Immediately after the commissioning ceremonies, we were again in dungarees and started loading stores [supplies]. These all-hands, loading parties were so impressive and tiring that to avoid them in the future was everyone's aim. [I got out of a few but not many.]

November 26, 1942—With two training crews aboard, we left NOB Norfolk on our shakedown cruise up and down the Chesapeake. Everything went pretty well. The crew is learning fast. Our radio transmitter conked out.

November 27, 1942—The Commander of our group of LSTs is on board, therefore, we have been designated flagship of the group. The radio transmitter is still acting up. Fired all guns for the first time. That three-inch gun in the back of the radio room sure shakes us up. I stood watch with the signalmen on the bridge. It is cold up there.

November 30, 1942—We are anchored off Solomons, Maryland. Technicians worked for hours and finally fixed our transmitter. We ran up and down, degaussing the ship today. This is a system of neutralizing the ship's magnetic field so we will not attract magnetic mines.

Most enlisted men seem to like the following poem, as they are conscious of the long noses of some Americans, especially girls and commissioned officers. In my opinion, the commissioned officer system is unjust as it would like to set up a caste system in which the enlisted man should feel inferior.

The Sailor Boy in Blue

Listen all you civies
who live along the shore,
Smile when you meet a sailor
as you never smiled before.

There are good and bad among them
in every single lot,
But they're a darn sight better
than the enemy you've got.

Should an enemy invade us
now that we're in the strife
Remember that the boy in blue
is the one who'll give his life.

So when you feel superior
to a man in uniform,
Remember what he stands for
Then, for heaven's sake—reform.

—ALLIE MAE JOSEPH

December 2, 1942—We are again anchored off Solomons, Maryland. There was some excitement when the liberty boat was overdue. I finally contacted radio Norfolk, and they determined that the boat was held up because of weather.

What I have seen of the shores of the Chesapeake Bay fascinates me. I would like to take a trip around the bay in a small boat. Some places along the shore look just like they belong in a novel. The sun coming up this morning was just beautiful.

December 6, 1942—We sailed up the Chesapeake to the navel college at Annapolis, Maryland today. Midshipmen swarmed all over this new strange-looking craft. They asked questions of us continuously as if we were experts. All the midshipmen seemed friendly and the type who will make good officers. It must be great to go to an outstanding school like this.

December 13, 1942—A dandy remote control unit was installed from the radio room to the wheelhouse. I managed to get myself assigned to this remote unit in the event of General Quarters [a call to get to assigned battle stations quickly]. I can see and hear what is going on when the ship goes into action.

December 24, 1942—At 3:25 A.M., I was given a shove by the Bos'n [boatswain] of the watch and told it was time to get ready for my watch. Very sleepy, I got up and relieved my man in the radio room. Nothing much came over.

In the morning, we had General Quarters. I am assigned to the inter-ship phones. I will have voice radio when the installation is complete. After General Quarters, fellow radioman Schellhorn and

I practiced taking radio bearings with the direction finder and then plotting them to find our position.

After anchoring in Norfolk Harbor, another LST tied alongside. An arrangement was made that the other ship would take over the radio watch for the night, and we would take over the signal watch. Christmas day the procedure would be reversed.

For the first time since we got the ship, all of the radiomen got liberty together. It was after 1700 that we climbed down the net on the side of the ship into the liberty boat which took us to NOB.

We took the trolley to Norfolk and wound up in a filthy beer joint on Granby Street. The four of us sat down in a booth and one of the waitresses, who frequently tried to flirt with us, said, "It is a fine thing when an American girl must go out with a limey sailor because Americans haven't any money." The truth is the American sailor is too smart to spend time with her type.

As the jukebox played "White Christmas," "Mr. Five by Five" [funny song about a man five-feet tall and five-feet wide], etc., I often thought of home and what my family was doing now. When they stopped serving beer at 10:30, in accordance with the law, we left the joint and tried to send a telegram of greetings home. Both Western Union and Postal Telegraph refused to take any more greetings. As we wandered up Granby Street, Christmas carols blared away from the loudspeaker on top of the Monticello Hotel. Everyone on the street sang some of them. Most of the people were half-drunken sailors.

We got a taxi to NOB and then walked a mile to the liberty wharf. We waited an hour in the cold for the liberty boat. When I got back to the ship, there was a good Christmas present waiting. Three packages and about ten letters had arrived. I went into one of the empty troop compartments and sat on one of the bunks and read my mail. About 2:30 A.M., I washed and turned in.

December 31, 1942—Today is New Year's Eve, and here I am out on the Chesapeake. We calibrated in the morning and then headed back to Little Creek, and I was on radio watch most of the afternoon. We anchored off Little Creek. I gathered from messages coming over the radio that we will practice beachings for the first time tomorrow.

January 1, 1943—When the New Year came, I found myself on radio watch all by myself. At midnight, an extra dash came over the air which indicated the New Year, then silence reigned. The signalman said that outside there was a lot of noise from shore. The ship anchored next to ours sent "Happy New Year" by blinker.

I thought I would get some news from the USA shortwave station, but when I turned the dial just off my frequency (I could still hear any signals for us), I didn't get a U.S. station but heard a German news broadcast in English. The speaker gave greetings from Hitler and said, "This is Germany calling." He signed off by saying, "This war is fought between two great forces—Jewish Bolshevism and the great new order. Why is America in the wrong camp?" At 4:00 A.M., I was relieved and got a few hours of sleep.

Our First Beaching

January 1, 1943—At about 8:30 A.M., battle condition 1M was called. Everyone ran to their posts. My station is on the voice phone in the wheelhouse where I keep the log. Here are some of the orders given and replies received during beaching procedures:

> *Undog the bow doors* was the first order given by Captain Browning who was at the conn from the signal bridge.
>
> *Guns report. Guns one, two, three, four, five, six, and stern guns manned and ready.*
>
> *Repair one and two manned and ready.*
>
> *Steam winch manned and ready.*
>
> *Emergency steering room manned and ready.*
>
> *Engines ahead two-thirds.*

The crew seemed a little anxious for we were the first of the ships to attempt a beaching. Twenty ships sat out in the Chesapeake Bay, half LSTs and half LCIs (Landing Craft, Infantry). Overhead, twelve Navy fighting planes maneuvered on which the gunners practiced sighting. A single, medium tank ran up and down the beach.

Forward ballast tanks filled and after tanks half-filled, sir, came the report.

Engines ahead one-third, right five-degree rudder. Forcastle take soundings and report.

Lower the ramp. Ramp lowered sir. Report soundings—by the mark three. Fly identification flags for beaching.

We moved in closer and headed straight for the beach. Another LST to our port then headed in.

Stern anchor standby. Drop stern anchor and keep line taut while letting out. Soundings by the mark two.

How much line left to be let out in stern?

About 150 feet, sir.

Engine stopped. Signalman prepare flags.

We saw the beach come closer and closer.

Main panel overheating. Helmsman, check the swing and head straight for the little black house on the shore.

Soundings by the mark one, sir.

She does not answer to the wheel, sir.

Ship is grounded, sir.

Anyone who could leave their post for a minute ran to the bow to see how we made out. The ship was about seventy-five feet from shore in approximately seven feet of water.

Engines two-thirds astern, pull in on stern anchor.

Slowly we eased off the beach.

Stop all engines. Stern anchor line believed fouled in propeller.

The captain ran to the stern, and I wondered if the sailors would free the rope or if it was really fouled. Ten minutes went by, and the ship finally cleared herself. We left the beach, and our first practice beaching had been a success.

After two more beachings, we went into port and tied to a buoy so some of the fellows could have liberty. Not me. I must stand a 2:00 A.M. to 4:00 A.M. watch.

January 6, 1943—I have found another vocation I will never follow. Doubt that I could be a tailor. A button came off my peacoat, and after much labor, I sewed the button back on. I stuck my finger many times before I finished. The hell of it is that, after all this work, when I put the coat on, all the buttons were out of line, and the coat didn't button properly. I am now in the process of trying to reset the button. I am glad there are no women around for I called the buttons some fancy names. I lost two of my best needles on the deck and can't find them. At least I didn't sew up my pocket again anyway.

For the next month, we continued to maneuver and practice landings with other LSTs on the Chesapeake. We all knew it was just a matter of time before we would be on our way overseas, and we wanted to be as prepared as possible.

February 6, 1943—We have been working very hard loading supplies at Norfolk. The ship is shipshape. I dropped my watch when the strap broke. I miss it a lot. Perhaps Mom can have it fixed if I send it home.

February 17, 1943—With five other LSTs, we sailed from Norfolk, heading for New York. About eight hours out, General Quarters was called. The convoy started zig zag maneuvers. The destroyer escorting us dropped depth chargers. *Was there really a German sub in the area?* Guess we will never know. The experience gave us all a funny feeling but I can't say that anyone seemed scared.

It was a thrill for me to enter New York Harbor past Ambrose Light, Sandy Hook and through the Narrows past Staten Island, my hometown. Many a Sunday while I was growing up, Dad took us down to Quarantine on the Staten Island side of the Narrows to watch the ships go in and out. There was always a steady stream of ships going in and out. Now I was on one of those ships entering the Harbor.

We docked at pier 90 (I think) on the west side of Manhattan and the Hudson River. Before too much delay, I received liberty and surprised everyone when I arrived home for the night. [This would be the last time I would see my family and my hometown for more than two years.]

Before joining the convoy for the trip overseas, we went to the Bayonne Naval Supply Depot on about February 20th where we had a 105 ft. LCT (Landing Craft, Tank) placed on our main deck for transport overseas. Two hundred Seabees came aboard, and our cargo deck was full to the brim with Seabee equipment. The Free French battleship FS *Richelieu* sat in the big grave dock next to us, signaling the wide world we would soon be a part of.

On the signal lights aboard USS *LST-388*.

The Long Voyage Across the Atlantic

W E NOW HAD OUR SHIP and the voyage across the Atlantic could begin. It was time to join the war. The crew seemed ready, possibly a little apprehensive, but mostly confident. This is what we had signed up for. This is how we chose to serve our Country. Now it was finally time to do just that. Our destination would be somewhere in Africa; where, we wouldn't learn until well underway.

February 23, 1943—We are finally on our way overseas with a crew of about 100 men. Also on board are about 200 Seabees with equipment to set up an amphibious base. Our convoy consists of five American and five British LSTs. We are being escorted by several destroyers. A blimp overhead helps guide us to the larger convoy because of the ground fog.

Even though loaded, our ship began a steady roll that kept up all across the Atlantic. Many men got seasick but I wasn't one of them. Sleeping did prove to be difficult however. Bermuda was to be our first landfall.

February 27, 1943—This evening at sunset, land was sighted. I went on deck to see the beautiful hills of Bermuda across a picturesque light blue-green sea. The captain had poor charts, so he didn't want to risk entering the harbor without a pilot. When we got close to Hamilton [capital of Bermuda], it was dark. We anchored on the lee [protected] side of the island. No sooner had we anchored than the ship bounced off the bottom. We easily backed off. A native pilot came aboard and guided us to a safe anchorage for the night.

February 28, 1943—This morning we tied up just inside the basin to a stone breakwater [a barrier built to protect a coast or harbor from waves]. The dockyard is not far from the town of Hamilton. The authorities are very strict and insist that we not use the ship's head [toilet]. We must go ashore and use the filthy British heads. No garbage of any kind can be thrown over the side. I only got three-quarters of an hour liberty. Liberty ended for everyone at 6:00 p.m.

March 1, 1943—We had good liberty this afternoon. We traveled to Hamilton on an old-fashioned ferry that looks as if it had been doing duty on the Thames River seventy-five years before it was sent to Bermuda. Several of us went sightseeing by bicycle along the cliffs and enjoyed the countryside. We stopped at a beautiful spot and drank and ate some of the things we had bought back in town. We talked of our intentions concerning returning here after the war. Way in the distance we could see the dockyard where the USS *LST-388* was docked, which reminded us that our liberty was almost up, so we headed back.

March 2, 1943—Many of the boys went swimming from the side of the ship today because only half the crew is allowed ashore at one time. I dove off the side of the ship and hit the water too hard with my head as I held my hands too high. What a whack on the old bean! I am lucky I didn't break my neck.

   This evening, I was slightly injured. We are not permitted to use the ships head, so I have to walk down the quay to shore latrines. Before turning in, a buddy and I decided to take the trip to the foot of the quay to relieve ourselves. It was dark and rainy. The path we followed went around a large open steam pit. We were walking and talking when all of a sudden I disappeared down into the steam pit. Someone forgot to put the cover over it. I think I was laughing and crying at the same time. There were scrapes and bruises all over

Ships Control group (or Bridge Crew). Starting from the right, I am in the back row, third sailor over, with the black watch cap.

me. I was ready to clobber the pharmacist mate who patched me up because he thought the whole incident very funny.

March 3, 1943—We sailed from Bermuda today and will not see land again for twenty-two days. Once well on our way, we found out our destination is to be Gibraltar.

It was overcast most of the crossing. The ship rolled continuously, making sleeping and eating difficult. I enjoyed the radio watches. Often, I would copy the news and tack it to the bulletin board for the crew to know what was going on in the world. We were not permitted to sleep in our bunks in the daytime. I read a lot or studied for the next rating. I wish I could have gotten interested in cards, but they were not my cup of tea. Many times I sat on the fantail [stern or back of the ship] and just watched the ocean and the wake given out by our powerful diesel engines. Sometimes a shipmate from New Orleans, Fernandez, would play the banjo.

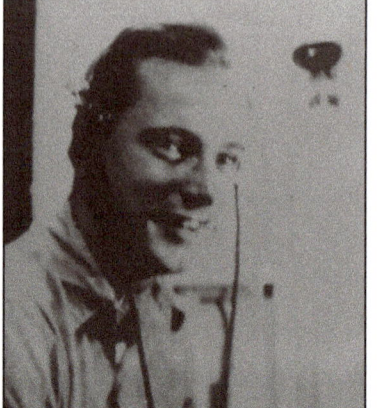

Left: In the radio room of the USS *LST-388*.

Above and left: Aboard ship.

Opposite: We were the original radiomen aboard the USS *LST-388*: Callie Leroy Stocks, myself, and Bill Schellhorn.

THE LONG VOYAGE ACROSS THE ATLANTIC

We had several submarine scares during the long voyage, but nothing developed. Submarine reports from NSS showed subs all around us but none within close range. The LCIs [landing craft, infantry] on the outside of our convoy could be mistaken as subs on the surface from a distance.

I became quite proficient at the signalman's job and often assisted at the blinker, semaphore, or flags. I could read the blinker and semaphore as well as any signalman and the signal flags used in maneuvering were rather easy. Signalmen must stay constantly alert, and they also have to put up with all kinds of weather. It didn't take long for me to garner a new respect for them.

Gibraltar

GIBRALTAR, a British territory sitting at the entrance to the Mediterranean Sea, just below Spain, had been established as Allied headquarters by Dwight D. Eisenhower in November of 1942. It served as the gateway to the Mediterranean, and to North Africa, and a port for many a sailor and soldier's first encounter with Europe.

March 25, 1943—We anchored off Gibraltar today. I was hoping for a freshwater shower again. The USS *LST-388* does not have a purifier, and thus, the 300 people on board have to conserve freshwater. Washing ourselves and our clothes in saltwater for twenty-two days made us real old salts.

When the fog lifted this morning, we saw before us the famous, huge mountain that seems to be made of solid rock. The cliffs and sides go almost straight up for about 1,400 feet. It looks impossible to capture. (Gibraltar's many guns control the entrance to the Mediterranean Sea.) To the rear of the fortress are the beautiful green hills of Spain. When the weather cleared, we saw across the strait to Morocco in Africa. Rumor has it that Oran, Algeria, is our next stop.

Some of the boys went on liberty this morning, and the rest of us will probably go tonight. It will be nice to see something besides the ship after so long at sea. On the way over, General Quarters was called once when a British ship reported seeing the wake of a torpedo. No one ever saw a submarine. When we docked last night, a big British sub docked alongside us.

I took a math test for radioman 2/c and got a mark of 3.3. The mark would have been higher if I didn't make some careless mistakes. No further mention has been made of my being made senior radioman.

March 26, 1943—The communications officer sent me ashore with the outgoing mail. It had to be delivered to the American Consul in Gibraltar. I had quite a time finding the place for it was up a small street and down a walk. After disposing of the mail, several of us stood in line at the American money exchange station.

This town is something out of a movie. The houses are as old as the hills and naturally Spanish in style. The streets are narrow and winding. Spaniards seem to run all commercial establishments. Every type of sailor and soldier in the Allied Forces is on liberty here. There are crowds everywhere.

I went on liberty with a Seabee who had been a rancher in Nevada before the war. We visited every place worthwhile in an hour and a half. They are all international dives. Several joints had all-girl orchestras. The music was a mixture of American and Spanish, and it sounded wonderful after so long a voyage. There were intriguing Spanish dancers at several places. The main street of this town is much worse than East Main Street in Norfolk, Virginia. Gibraltar is a great port for a sailor to have a fling. We loved it.

Our short stay in Gibraltar revived us after such a long journey at sea. It had been exhilarating to be among so many different soldiers and sailors, to be past the training and now be overseas.

On board ship. Shipmate Glenn, myself and my Communications Officer, Lt. Donald B. McKnight.

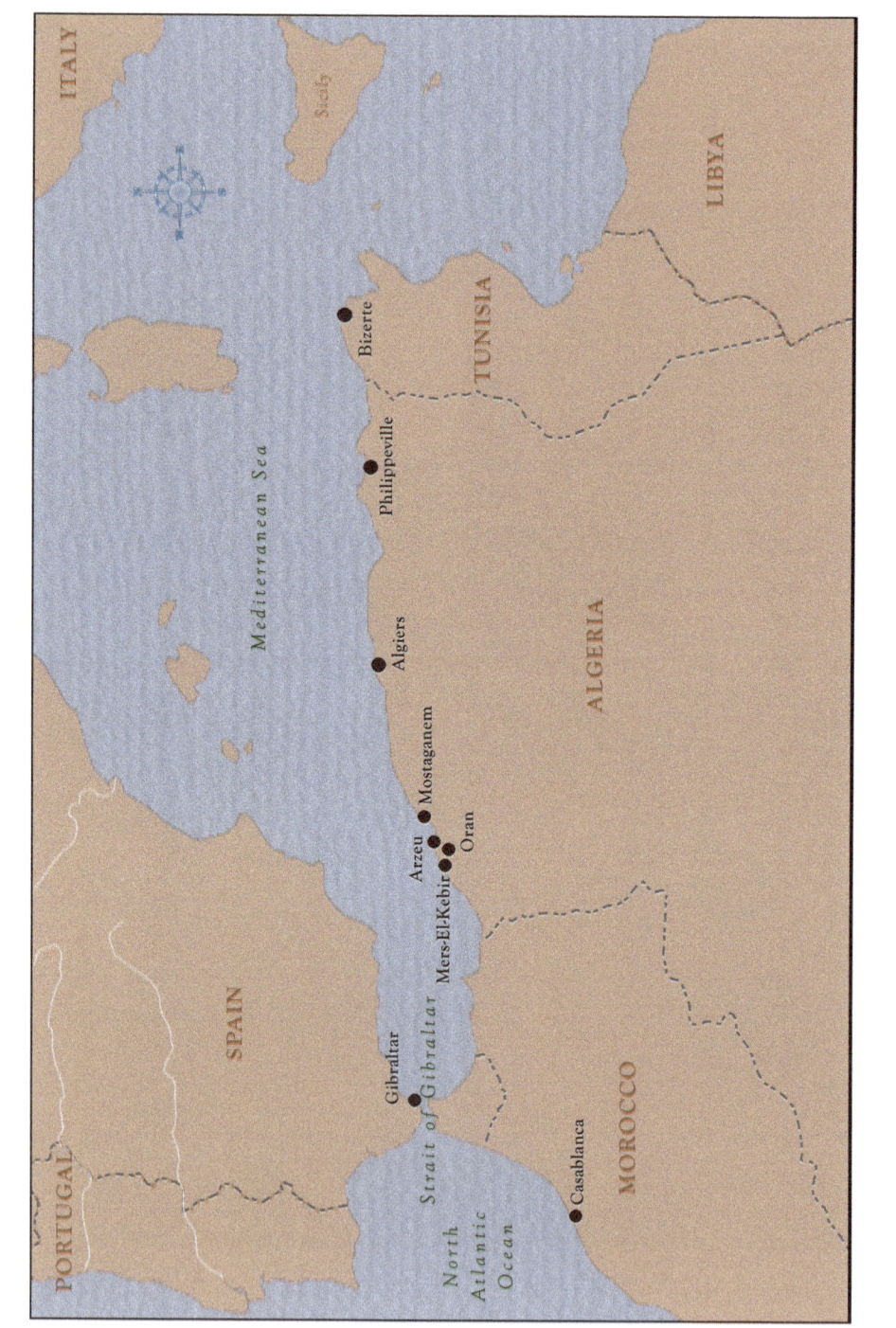

North Africa and the Mediterranean

WHEN FRANCE FELL TO THE GERMANS in 1940, Germany gained control of the French empire, which included North Africa. The Allies needed control of this region for many reasons, one of which was to establish Allied bases to stock with troops, vehicles, guns, ammunition, and supplies for the coming invasions into German-occupied Europe.

On November 8, 1942, Allied combat troops landed at several locations, including beaches near Casablanca in French Morocco, and near Oran and Algiers in Algeria. The invasions, all falling under the code name of *Operation Torch*, were the first amphibious combat landings to take place. However, no LSTs had been completed or available in time to participate, so only smaller landing craft had been used.

We arrived in North Africa not long after the execution of *Operation Torch*. The majority of the captured ports were greatly damaged either by war action, or deliberately damaged by fleeing French, Italian, or German forces. Salvage crews and engineers had been brought in for this reason and went to work clearing and repairing the ports. By the time we arrived, these repairs were still ongoing and new bases still being established.

Algeria

Algeria contained three new Allied naval bases—Oran, Mers-el-Kebir and Arzeu. Oran's harbor, although badly damaged, became the most important operating and supply base in the region. Mers-el-Kebir, a small town just three miles to the west of Oran, provided a small military harbor. Arzeu, twenty-five miles to the east of Oran, became a training base for amphibious operations. There were also minor ports, such as those at Mostaganem and Philippeville. We would spend time in all of them.

> *March 27, 1943*—We left Gibraltar, heading for Port Arzeu in Algeria today. There were two General Quarters alerts on the way, but nothing happened. Porpoises followed us a good way across the Mediterranean Sea to Africa.
> The stay in Arzeu was only a few hours, and we were off for the city of Oran. On leaving, we almost upset the small tug that helped pull us from our berth. The Frenchmen were running up and down, yelling for us to turn them loose. The line had become too taut for them to cast it off. We were dragging the tug sideways.

Oran, Algeria, is an impressive-looking city as seen from the sea. It is situated on a high bluff. Only ten percent of the crew could go on liberty at any one time. What most of us remember about this port is the long steps up from the waterfront and our first experience with drinking vino. I never saw anyone get so drunk on wine as did some of our crew. It was a joke how they rolled, walked, or were carried back to the ship.

As the clearing of ports continued, ships maneuvered as best they could. Yet each port and harbor had their challenges. Big LSTs were not always the easiest to maneuver.

> *April 15, 1943*—While entering Mostaganem harbor, the wind pushed us into the harbor net and fouled a propeller and the rudder. Mostaganem is a fair-sized city, but the harbor is one of the smallest. A diver from the salvage tug Lapwing finally got us untangled.

North Africa-Mostaganem Postcard.

We made a practice landing with the soldiers last week. We were in a mock battle, landing trucks at the mouth of a river. It was a success but the way planes swooped out of nowhere convinced us we need lots of protection while unloading.

While our main base seemed to be Arzeu, we went up and down the Algerian coast visiting Philippeville, Mostaganem, and Mers-El-Kébir near Oran often to carry cargo or on a training mission. There were numerous air raids that disturbed our sleep but none in much force. Most of our casualties came from flak falling back down from our own anti-aircraft fire. I was glad to be assigned to a radio (voice) in the wheelhouse during General Quarters so that I could see and hear what was going on.

Liberties, or authorized leaves, while in these ports were a welcome relief. During one particular liberty while in Arzeu, sometime around *May 3, 1943*, I had a heart-pounding experience. There was a vaudeville show given by some French entertainers in an old movie theater. Ninety-nine percent of the audience was American soldiers. The only seat left was in the front row. The show proved to be naughty but good. A very pretty singer/dancer came sauntering onto the stage. She was dressed in black short-shorts, black stockings, black jacket, high heels, high hat, and carried a cane, which she twirled as she sang. What a beautiful body. While she sang, she took most of her clothes off. I was embarrassed but thrilled. The soldiers whistled and screamed. While singing, she came down the aisle, patting the soldiers' heads. To my astonishment, she came up to me, patted me on the head, then kissed me. Boy, did I blush! The soldiers howled and several shined their flashlights on us. [These many years later the scene is as fresh in my memory as if it were yesterday.]

There was another source of entertainment in the small town of Arzeu which I didn't have guts enough to take advantage of. There was a legal whorehouse. The Army had medics stationed at the exit to make sure all US servicemen who were serviced there took a pro [prophylactic].

Tunisia

While we were moving in and out of the ports of Algeria, fierce fighting continued in the neighboring country of Tunisia. It would prove to be a challenge to conquer, but the Allied troops prevailed and captured the key cities of Tunis and Bizerte in early May 1943. With this conquest, the Allies gained a number of usable ports and air bases, imperative to the coming invasions planned for Sicily and the Italian mainland. Bizerte would soon become very important to us, as it was to be the staging point for both invasions the USS *LST-388* was to participate in in the region.

> *May 13, 1943*—We reached Bizerte, Tunisia, [the northernmost city in Africa] at noon. Sunken ships are everywhere. Not far from us a big liner [transport] lays on its side. The city is deserted and in ruins. Quite a few prisoners are on shore being loaded into LCIs [landing craft, infantry]. This port was taken by the Americans just a few days ago, May 8th. As of today, May 13th, all resistance on Cape Bon, Tunisia, ceased. German General von Armin was captured along with 250,000 Italian and German soldiers.

Thousands of German prisoners have been loaded onto LST ships near us for shipment to prison camps down the line. They seem well dressed. Some of their officers show overbearing ways. The way one of them walked around I began to wonder, who is the prisoner? These prisoners thought the Germans were still in Casablanca.

The capture of Casablanca, in French Morocco, had been part of *Operation Torch*. News of its fall in November of 1942, some six months prior to their capture, apparently had not reached these prisoners.

May 14, 1943—All the Seabees left the ship when we tied up to the wharf, nose-in, at the ruined former French air and seaplane base. A dozen or more LSTs unloaded at the same time. There are wrecked planes and hangers all about. I managed to sneak ashore with several others, and we walked into the deserted city. It is really off-limits. Not a house in the city seems worth repairing. Not a civilian in sight.

We walked many blocks, going into hotels, stores, houses, churches, etc. The city must have been quite prosperous before the war. Most buildings are just walls now, and we wondered how many bodies were buried under the debris. The main streets have been cleared, but the side streets and walks are just piles of rubble.

I shall never forget one huge church we entered. The beautiful steeple still rose above but was full of shell holes, and parts of it were missing altogether. There were really only two walls to the place. The center of the church was piled twenty-five feet high with rock and debris. In one corner of the church, a small altar was still standing, around which were some old chairs. Someone had had a service there soon after the battle. There were lovely statues and paintings, mostly in ruins. A huge pipe organ looked all smashed up, and the balcony on which it stood was now exposed to the weather, with no roof or walls around it. Six of us entered the church. We all removed our hats, and I believe most of us said a prayer to ourselves. None of us dared take anything for a souvenir although there were valuables all around.

In many houses, there were toys and pictures and remains of what must have been nice homes. There were pictures of happy families and gatherings in almost every house. If anyone could read French, there were millions of expensively bound books and periodicals laying around.

Not a dock in the harbor is left in one piece. Huge barrage balloons [large blimp-like balloons designed to prevent aircraft attack] hover over the demolished city.

May 17, 1943—We left Bizerte with a load of tanks, heading for Philippeville, Algeria. It is easier to transport troops and equipment by LST than to use the poor roads.

May 21, 1943—We had liberty for a few hours in Philippeville. I enjoyed myself even though I had the leery feeling that the French soldiers and civilians did not seem to be too friendly. Many of them just stared at us as if to say, "What the hell do you want here?" Another fellow and I went on liberty together. We walked up and down the main street and bought a few souvenirs.

By chance, we met two soldiers who we had taken from Bizerte to Philippeville. They took us to a place where we bought a lot of champagne. There was an old Spaniard there who fought for the Loyalists in the Spanish Civil War. He took us to a place where there was to be a movie, but we couldn't get in. We then went to an Arab restaurant in the heart of the Arab district where we had bread, soup, and beans. The place had little light, and the fixtures were wooden and old. We picked up three more soldiers by this time, and the seven of us sat together. The eats were better than I expected.

The soldiers, most of whom came from Texas, were very friendly. They had been in Africa since the allied invasion and had participated in the battles of Mateur and Bizerte. They told us about the German soldiers and how the American infantry showed no mercy. Few individual prisoners were taken. They told of many Germans killed after shell fragments had sprayed them from overhead. The dead Germans would be still sitting, holding their rifles, and the soldiers would just fill the hole they were sitting in with dirt.

The soldiers had been eating c-rations for a long time. They admitted how scared they were in the battles and how they quickly learned to pray. All of them liked the French girls but could not get many of them to look at them.

We tried to buy some of the Arab silverware that had Arab designs on it, but the old Arab boss with the round, red hat wouldn't let us. I obtained a German rifle which everyone says is very good. I don't know what I will do with it.

May 25, 1943—We are back in Oran. The trip back here was almost like a cruise—the water beautiful and calm, surrounded by gorgeous mountain scenery, balmy weather with hardly a cloud in the sky; and no soldiers or Seabees to bother us. We sat on the fantail and listened to phonograph records and talked. Every so often while underway, we spotted dead bodies. There must be an awful lot of dead in these waters. The several mines we came across were used for target practice.

We have not had ice cream, fresh milk, real potatoes, or fresh meat since leaving the States. Spam and powdered eggs are a staple. The coffee tastes like it is made of chopped-up rubber bands.

May 26, 1943—Heard today that Arzeu was bombed last night, and the anti-aircraft unit on the breakwater was a victim of a direct hit. We often went swimming off this breakwater. I understand the casualties were high.

I learned that a hometown friend, Jack Horan, is a lieutenant on USS *LST-355*, now at Arzeu, so I hitched a ride in an Army truck to Arzeu. This trip of about fifty miles was my first inland sojourn since I came to Africa. It was great to see so many nice-looking farms. The hayfields and rolling hills reminded me of some parts of the United States. When I met Jack, he took me into the officers' quarters to his room. We had a wonderful time together catching up.

You can't compare the officer's life with the enlisted men. We sleep three bunks on top of each other, twelve or more to a compartment. I sleep on a top bunk with the general alarm bell at my feet. When the alarm goes off, it shakes me up for several minutes. It is a wonder I don't have a heart attack.

When I returned to Oran by Army truck, there were only ten minutes to spare before catching the liberty boat back to the ship.

June 22, 1943—Two LSTs, the -333 and the -387, which crossed the Atlantic with us and are usually part of our group, were torpedoed by the German submarine U-593 while en route to Bizerte. They were carrying troops specially trained to fight fires. Forty-five men were killed, and seventy-five were injured. The USS *LST-333* had to be beached and abandoned. USS LCT-208 [landing craft, tank] was also lost. [The USS *LST-387* was towed into Bizerte on July 4, 1943, in almost sinking condition. Three radiomen buddies I had gone through training at Little Creek and Solomons with were killed.]

June 27, 1943—For the past month, we have been up and down the African coast, transporting army and navy supplies. In between these trips, we practice maneuvers for an invasion.
I passed all tests for RM 2/C and hope to be rated soon.

At Arzeu, the Seabees put huge pontoon causeways on the sides of our ship. When we hit the invasion shore, the Seabees will maneuver the pontoons to the front of our bow doors to facilitate unloading along the shallow beaches.

June 29, 1943—We are still docked, nose-in, at the old French airport and seaplane base loading cargo. I managed to get ashore here again and looked over the many wrecked planes, etc. Not a hanger or building was left unscathed at this base.

The salvage tug Redwing, which helped us out several times, was sunk by a mine. She sank today outside Bizerte.

Everything seems set for the invasion of Sicily. There are hundreds of ships anchored in Lake Bizerte. We have had at least one air raid every night lately. There have been thirteen alerts in the last two days.

During these air raids, the German flares give me a strange feeling; they have what I call a 'fearsome serenity'. They are extremely bright and seem to doze in the air, hung there by skyhooks. For a spell, the flares defy the laws of gravity. They burn bright enough to cast a shadow on the bridge, which up to now, would be in darkness. These sky lamps seem to stay on for what would be an eternity, almost without moving. When at last, the light fades, another sky lamp bursts into light some yards below the first.

June 30, 1943—The list of those to be rated today was posted on the bulletin board, and my name was first. But...catch-22! Since some small stores [supplies], which we were carrying to Bizerte, were stolen, all ratings have been stopped. Tough break for me since I had nothing to do with the stolen goods.

The Luftwaffe (German air force), observing the great concentration of ships here at Bizerte, subjects us to many night air raids. In the past few weeks, we have had several casualties from our own flak during these air raids. When all the ships open up, the flak falls on the deck like rain. A friend of mine is in very bad shape after a piece of shrapnel struck him in the head and went through his helmet into his skull. He had been assigned to the bow anti-aircraft gun.

The chief bos'n mate received a piece of shrapnel in his hind-end. If the old grouch had stayed at his damage control post instead of stepping out on deck during the raid, he would be able to sit down right now.

When that three-inch gun on our stern goes off, it almost knocks me across the wheelhouse.

July 4, 1943—The USS *LST-387* was towed into Bizerte today and we now have the full story of what happened. On this ship, four out of five radiomen were killed, and on the USS *LST-333* one, and possibly two, radiomen were killed. Large total loss of life on both ships. USS *LST-333* is a total wreck on a beach and USS *LST-387*, although towed in, is a total loss.

The three fellows who I knew best among the dead were Scampoli, Unsworth and Morhan. Scampoli, who slept next to me at Little Creek and Solomons, had been a pal for almost a year. Unsworth and Morhan were on the USS *LST-388* (my ship) on our first trip to Bizerte. Both were swell fellows. Scampoli died in the hospital. Part of Unsworth's skull was found. No trace of Morhan was found. Some horrible stories have been told of the torpedoings. Three quarters of the engineers on the *LST-387* are dead besides four of the five radiomen.

Unfortunately, this wouldn't be the last LSTs, or their crews, lost in the war. The coming months would dually earn the LST their nicknames of *Large Slow Target* when in motion, and *Large Stationary Target* when beached.

North Africa, by this time, had become crowded with Allied troops, ships, and equipment, all in preparation for the coming invasions. Wherever there were accessible beaches, we were holding exercises. All the ports overflowed with supplies.

Joint army-navy training exercises intensified in the waters and beaches surrounding Lake Bizerte, with full-scale dress rehearsals of the coming invasion into Sicily.

The goal was to first land assault troops, quickly followed by landing tanks and antitank guns. This was the LST's main function, along with the smaller LCTs. We would do this by unloading troops onto the smaller crafts while still out at sea, and then grounding ourselves on the beaches and lowering our bow ramp to expel needed tanks, vehicles, and guns, either directly on the beach or over pontoon causeways.

Assault loading of LSTs with tanks, vehicles, troops, and supplies really required a huge effort. It involved loading on the same ship not only the troops, but the needed equipment, vehicles, and supplies for those particular troops. All of these needed to be arranged for unloading in an order necessary to meet tactical situations immediately upon hitting the beach.

American war correspondent Ernie Pyle described those last days in Bizerte before the invasion of Sicily like this:

> We weren't told what day we were to sail, but it was obvious it wasn't going to be immediately for there was still too much going and coming, too much hustle and bustle about the port. The activity of invasion preparation was so seething, those last few weeks, that in practically every port in North Africa the harbor lights blazed, contemptuous of danger, throughout the night. There simply wasn't time to be cautious. The ship loading had to go on, so they let the harbor lights burn.[2]

NORTH AFRICA AND THE MEDITERRANEAN

M4 Sherman tanks being loaded onto LSTs for Operation Husky, Bizerte, Tunisia, 7 Jul 1943 (Source: United States National Archives).

LSTs in Bizerte, preparing for Operation Husky (Invasion of Sicily).

Invasion of Sicily

WE SAILED ON PAST the breakwater with the waves beating against it and out onto the dark blue of the Mediterranean. The wind was freshening and far away mist began to form on the watery horizon. Suddenly we were aware of a scene that will shake me every time I think of it the rest of my life. It was our invasion fleet, formed there far out at sea, waiting for us.

There is no way of conveying the enormous size of that fleet. On the horizon, it resembled a distant city. It covered half the skyline, and the dull-colored camouflaged ships stood indistinctly against the curve of the dark water, like a solid formation of uncountable structures blending together. Even to be a part of it was frightening. I hope no American ever has to see its counterpart sailing against us.
—ERNIE PYLE, from his book, *Brave Men*[3]

THE ISLAND OF SICILY sits less than three miles from the southern tip of Italy and would be the site of the first Allied invasion into German-occupied Europe. American troops would land on the beaches surrounding three locations -Licata, Gela and Scoglitti. The British and Canadians would land in the southeast, near the town of Syracuse.

The USS *LST-388* joined the Allied forces gathered on Lake Bizerte, on the north coast of Tunisia, in early July 1943, in preparation for the invasion, code named HUSKY. We would sail with the *Joss Force Attack Groups*, destined for the beaches closest to Licata, Sicily. Our designated beach was *Blue Beach*, Licata.

"Pontoons of Platoon J of the 1006 Seabees, secured alongside *LST-388* on the run into BLUE BEACH, Licata." Source: *Building the Navy's Bases in World War II: History of the Bureau of Yards and Docks and the Civil Engineer Corps, 1940–1946.*

July 4–5, 1943—We loaded the Army vehicles together with tons of ammunition on our top deck and pulled into Lake Bizerte. The lake held hundreds of ships, and the night shone clear with numerous stars. Most of us were not quite sure whether this was the real thing or another dry run. About eleven at night, I was sleeping soundly when the General Quarters alarm went off. I ran to my battle station in the wheelhouse as fast as possible. When I got there, every ship around was firing tracers, and searchlights streaked skyward. The enemy planes flew high. A destroyer on our starboard side let go with all she had, and a German plane started to fall. It looked as if it were headed straight for our ship but crashed just astern of us. When it hit the water, it erupted in a mass of flames. Another plane fell a short distance off. We had three shrapnel casualties, none very serious—one officer and two enlisted men.

July 6–7, 1943—We loaded more army [soldiers] and proceeded outside the harbor for the night. At dawn, the great armada was formed. On top deck, we had tons of ammunition chained down for the Army, and landing pontoons stretched the full length on both sides of the ship. A barrage balloon tended by a limey floated overhead, attached to a big vent. There were ships of every description heading out. The sky was clear and the water choppy.

Off the bay of Tunis, we met more ships. Planes continually flew overhead. After we passed Pantelleria [Italian island in the Strait of Sicily] and almost to Malta, the water started to get rough. As we headed into the waves, the cargo-laden USS *LST-388* shuddered and shook from stem to stern like a springboard. The wind began to blow. The LCIs [landing craft infantry] were more like submarines because they rode over one wave and under the next.

The LCIs went into Sousse [Tunisia] for the night, but we kept going. We arrived at Malta too late for a planned rendezvous, so we continued on. In the wind, our balloon snapped its wire and went up, up, up, until she burst.

The beaches of southern Sicily were not amenable to LSTs running onto the beach and unloading. Most of the area was filled with *false beaches*, sandbars with enough water over them to float a landing craft or LCT [landing craft, tank] but not big LSTs. The terrain was hazardous; a tunnel lay between the false and real beach, forming "a miniature lagoon deep enough to drown a tank". The answer to this was the Seabees' pontoon causeway, assembled in Arzeu [Algeria] and carried on the side of the LSTs.[4]

On the night of July 9, 1943, things began to happen. We lay several miles off the Sicilian coast near Licata. The big ships threw shell after shell onto the shore. Shore batteries [fortified emplacement for heavy guns] opened up, and enemy aircraft came out to challenge us. Our big guns didn't take very long to silence the shore batteries. Several shells from shore hit close to us. Enemy planes made desperate trips over our ships but were driven off. At daylight, troops began to land from small boats.

We lowered our ramp and let out the Army amphibious trucks called ducks or DUKWs. This two-and-a-half-ton truck was designed both to "swim in the water and roll on land." It could drive to shore with its own propeller, then roll inland on its wheels. This was the first time these trucks were being used and no one knew whether they would be successful or not.[5]

Because of the rolling sea and poor ramp chains, our ramp gave way and fell down, under the water. The tank deck started to flood faster than our pumps could pump it out. Six inches of water flooded the tank deck. Making a super effort, two men dove down and attached cables to the ramp, and it was partially raised.

We were ordered into the beach at all speed. Our cargo of guns was vital! The pontoons rode on our sides after being dropped into the water. The Seabee handlers rode them in. As we hit the beach, the pontoons kept going and were fastened to the ramp. We were one of the first LSTs to beach and had little trouble unloading our guns over the pontoons.

We then pulled out to unload the ammunition into LCTs. All hands that could be spared from battle stations helped. Troughs were built and put over the side allowing ammunition to slide down to the LCT. I was sent to help. I worked until I felt I couldn't lift any more.

During the first day of unloading, we had a bombing attack every half hour. The planes would come out from around a mountain and be gone in a matter of seconds. I was on an LCT stacking shells when a bomb hit so close in the water that we all were splashed. Another plane strafed the ship and dropped a bomb that just missed our bow. I happened to look where the USS *LST-158* was unloading on the beach—the same spot where we had unloaded our guns. A plane swooped down the mountain and scored a direct hit with a bomb amidships. Within seconds a huge ball of fire and clouds of smoke rose high in the sky. The casualties must have been high.

Just down the way at Gela, other LSTs were also in trouble. USS *LST-338* and USS *LST-344* had to beach earlier than expected for the need of their guns and vehicles was so great. While unloading over their pontoon causeway, they were greatly hindered not only by strong current but by gunfire and shells falling all around them. Fortunately, neither were hit. Another LST, the USS *LST-313*, was not so lucky. As the sun was setting, USS *LST-313* was helping USS *LST-311* rig

Unloading a Battery of Anti-Aircraft Guns over a pontoon causeway in Sicily.

a pontoon causeway on the beach. The USS *LST-313* carried fully gassed-up "trucks, jeeps, halftracks, and ambulances", along with land mines, ammunition, and 37mm guns. A German Me-109 fighter aircraft loaded with bombs approached and targeted the USS *LST-313*. One bomb exploded below her tank deck and turned the ship "into a raging inferno"—a "death trap" for some. "Fortunately, her ramp was down", and they were able to pass many wounded men ashore. USS *LST-311* abandoned her pontoon causeway (which was blown apart) and swung around, placing her bow against the USS *LST-313*'s burning stern, helping save "about eighty men trapped" there.[6]

Only after we finished unloading on July 11, 1943, did we receive our first meal since starting the invasion. An emergency call from the beach for medical supplies was received, and our crew loaded these onto an LCT for delivery.

We joined a convoy back to Africa the night of July 11, 1943. The ship was underway for about an hour when the convoy was violently attacked by enemy aircraft. The USS *LST-388* had fallen a little behind, so they seemed to pick on our ship. I could hear the whistle of the bombs. Enemy planes came so close to the main deck that I could have thrown a stone and hit one. We ran a zig-zag course at flank speed [true maximum speed] and got into position in the convoy. First the planes came from up high and then low along the water. After this attack, all was quiet until we got back to Bizerte. I finally got a little sleep.

Later, I discovered this account given in *History of United States Naval Operations in World War II, Volume 9, Sicily-Salerno-Anzio, January 1943–June 1944* by Samuel Eliot Morison as to what happened that night of July 11–12.[7]

> That night, 11–12 July, was hellish in appearance and in fact. A heavy pall of smoke from burning *Robert Rowan* hung over the water, a perfect shield for enemy bombers against anti-aircraft fire; and the light from her fires silhouetted the ships in the roadstead. As if to avenge their stinging repulse on the ground that day, the Germans staged their heaviest air raid between 2150 and 2300. All ships got under way as the bombs began to drop; tracer bullets laced the sky; parachute flares lit up the scene. And, on top of this, came the American transport planes. In order to escape anti-aircraft fire of the Army ashore, which was very severe, the pilots tried to save themselves and their passengers by flying out over the roadstead at low altitude, right in the midst of the German bombing attack. Recognition signals were of no avail in the smoke- and tracer-filled night sky. Stricken planes plummeted into the sea and onto the land.
>
> All the next day paratroop survivors were trickling into Gela. Twenty-three of the 144 planes failed to return and over half of those which did return were badly damaged; 60 pilots and crewmen were lost, in addition to those passengers who were drowned or shot down.

Over the next several weeks, we continued to transport troops, ammunition, and equipment in accordance with the landing tables, which designated what troops and supplies went ashore, and when. We traversed the waters between Bizerte and Sicily amidst German U-boats, which continued to hunt for Allied ships in the waters surrounding the island. The German Luftwaffe continued their hunt by air. Before we knew it, we had made eight trips to Sicily carrying reinforcements, tanks, vehicles, equipment, and supplies.

The German Luftwaffe knew where the supplies and reinforcements were coming from, and on the night of August 17–18, there were two raids by Ju-88s [German combat planes] on Bizerte. An LCI was sunk, three vessels damaged, and some oil installations destroyed.

> *August 25, 1943*—We have been lying in Lake Bizerte for several days. Yesterday, we practiced beachings with pontoons which proved fairly successful. The USS *LST-388* has made five trips to Licata [Sicily], including the invasion, and then three trips to Palermo [Sicily] carting the Army with its equipment. Our only casualty on these trips has been our silverware. The Army carted most of it away.
>
> Palermo is a large and beautiful city; much different than anything we saw in Africa. There is evidence of heavy bombing, and the harbor is full of sunken ships. Most of the civilians are still in town. The death toll from the bombings must have been terrific! They live under such dreadful conditions. I saw many of them cooking their food outdoors on rocks and debris from ruins of neighboring buildings. Strange as it may seem, the Sicilian people seemed exceptionally glad to be conquered by the Americans.
>
> After returning to Bizerte, we had several air raids. During one bad raid, we had a serious casualty on the bow. The second loader was hit in the head by shrapnel and is in bad shape. His name is Moffa from Altoona, Pennsylvania, a most likeable fellow who talks of home and church. He invited us all to his home sometime for some good Italian spaghetti. I sure hope he lives! The next night, we had another raid and another casualty. This time Bailey on number two gun was hit in the leg.

Once Palermo, Sicily had been captured, it became an Allied port for further operations on the island, and eventually for the invasion of the Italian mainland. This photo shows the barrage balloons that protected the ships from divebombing attacks. They could be flown at different altitudes.

Yesterday two new officers came aboard, one line officer and the other a Navy doctor. The line officer tells me that he has only been over here a week and that there are ten new LSTs in the convoy. Something is up; possibly a new invasion very soon. Many of us think it is Southern Italy and are anxious to get on with it.

A new phonograph system and one hundred records have arrived from the States. The boys are having a heck of a good time listening

```
U.S.S. L.S.T. 388 COMMUNICATION SERVICE 7/20/43
ORIGINATOR:   COMMANDER TASK FORCE 86        201359B
ADDRESSEE:    ALL SHIPS THIS CIRCUIT

THE FOLLOWING EXCERPT FROM A PERSONAL
MESSAGE FROM PRIME MINISTER CHURCHILL
TO GENERAL EISENHOWER IS QUOTED FOR
INFORMATION AND PUBLICATION . QUOTE
FURTHER CONGRATULATIONS ON THE UNFOLDING SUCCESS OF THE
SICILIAN CAMPAIGN. THE WEATHER GAVE OCCASION ACCORDING
TO REPORTS MADE BY THE BRITISH ADMIRALTY FOR A MAGNIFICENT
DISPLAY OF AMERICAN SEAMANSHIP UNQUOTE.
```

Communication from Churchill to Eisenhower July 20, 1943; received aboard ship.

to the records. Wish we could have movies and beer for once. Our reward after each trip has been some mail from home and a bowl of ice cream.

Stories of the Sicilian invasion are now leaking out, and it seems that everything at Gela, just down the way from Licata, didn't go so well. The Germans almost drove the Americans into the sea. They were saved by American cruisers who took a bead on the German tanks and destroyed many of them. The Germans had 88s (88-mm anti-tank guns) on railway cars, but the cruisers, with the help of its observation plane, made short work of them.

Down the beach at Gela, not only were the LSTs in trouble, the troops on the beach encountered strong resistance by a German counterattack. A procession of tanks advanced on the beachhead by way of two different roads. Navy ships lay close into shore and bombarded the shore with their guns. This was the first use of such sea fire power and a defining moment in the war for our Navy.

August 27, 1943—Yesterday, a buddy and I went to Ferryville, which lies along the shore of Lake Bizerte. The docks and harbor are strewn with wreckage. The bow of a large submarine is sticking out of the water as if reaching for the stars. After reaching the town, we decided to take a trip to Tunis, which is in the British zone. We hitched rides from army trucks. All along the road, the devastation could be seen. We passed a lot of wrecked German equipment—tanks, trucks, guns, and a number of planes. Tunis is a large city, and the old Roman aqueduct we went under runs for eighty miles. We saw as much of the city as we could in a scant two hours. We saw the walled city and part of the ancient city of Carthage.

On the return trip, we got rides almost all the way by British lories [trucks]. At one time, we had to walk for half an hour before getting a lift. I didn't mind since a British Army lad walked with us. As we passed German wreckage and the British airfield, we saw many German graves. The British lad said, "that is the kind of Jerries I like to see—dead ones." He told us he hated the Germans because he had gone through the terrific German bombings of London and had seen his friends killed. He seemed only about twenty. When we reached a wrecked German Big Mark V1 tank, he left us and crossed the field to his camp. Several times he expressed his profound hatred for war. A swell chap if ever there was one. We reached Ferryville just minutes before the liberty boat departed.

We spent almost two months supplying Sicily with everything possible, with very little time off. By the end of August, the Allies had achieved their goal and the entire island was taken. The first large scale amphibious assault landing, using a combination of the new Landing Ship Tanks (LSTs), smaller landing craft, and the Army DUKWS, had been a success.

In his book, *Closing the Ring*, Winston Churchill stated this in reference to the supplying of the Sicilian invasion without the use of major ports on the island:

This was successful largely because of the new amphibious load-carrier, the American D.U.K.W., and even more the "landing ship, tank" (L.S.T.). This type of vessel had first been conceived and developed in Britain in 1940. A new design, based on British experience, was thereafter built in large numbers in the United States, and was first used in Sicily. It became the foundation of all our future amphibious operations, and was often their limiting factor.[8]

With the capture of Sicily complete, and air and navy bases established on the island, the Allies turned their eyes northward, to the mainland of Italy. To attack there would hopefully serve three purposes—to eliminate Italy from the war, engage as many German divisions as possible, and draw German forces away from France, which was the site of the next massive Allied invasion.

Little did we all know at the time, that, as naval historian Morison accurately describes, the landings at Salerno in Italy would soon make the Sicilian landings "seem like a summer picnic."[9]

Invasion at Salerno
Operation Avalanche

THE ALLIED INVASION of the Italian mainland focused mainly on Salerno, an area located in the southwestern part of the country, just south of Naples. There the Italian beach arcs for about 12 miles, with the town of Salerno at its North end. The British Division would attack by way of the northern beaches, and the American Division would attack through the southern beaches. My ship, the USS *LST-388*, loaded with British troops, would land at *Uncle Green Beach,* in the north. Once again, we were in Bizerte [Tunisia], preparing.

September 5, 1943—After getting pontoons on our sides, we loaded British troops and equipment. They are lads from the Eighth and First Armies, and all of them are well armed. We have four extra 40mm guns and two 20mm on top deck belonging to them. They are very different from American troops—not as well dressed or as healthy looking. Their food is far inferior to ours. I hated the way some of them looked at our chow when we went by with our trays. We all should have eaten the same.

September 7, 1943—Last night we proceeded outside the harbor and anchored in the Bizerte roads in preparation for getting underway at daylight. There was quite a large air raid by over 150 enemy planes. A terrific barrage went up, and several planes were shot down. A smoke screen was quickly laid down and there was no damage to any ship. The radio this morning said eight planes were downed, but I don't recall seeing that many. Perhaps our fighters caught them on the way back.

Port and starboard watches have been set, which means four hours on and four off. This is my second midnight-to-four watch in a row. I understand General Quarters will be called at midnight tomorrow night. It is very hot, and sleeping is difficult in crew's quarters. My compartment is right above the engine room, with poor ventilation.

These English chaps seem to be real nice fellows. The other night, a buddy and I were talking to two of their officers who were really intelligent men and have been in the war a long time. They were from the Eighth Army and told us of the campaign in the desert, the fall of France, and the terrific bombing of London.

One can hardly believe how terribly weak England was after the fall of France. Soldiers have told me that they were expected to hold their positions on coastal defenses with only a few rounds of ammunition or their rifle butts. They all felt Germany could have conquered Britain with a few thousand airborne troops if Hitler had only sent them. The RAF [Royal Air Force] was practically extinct. German raiders came over unmolested. All the British could do was sit there and take it because they didn't have many anti-aircraft guns. The situation was the same in Africa where Benghazi and Tobruk [Libya] were leveled. The Germans came over in their old-fashioned, three-motored crates to drop their bomb loads. All soldiers say the German is a first-class fighting man.

The BBC news broadcast states that the Naples area has been heavily bombed again. I certainly hope this is true, and military objectives are well battered before we land tomorrow night. Our convoy consists of LSTs, SCs, MSs, and several old British warships.

September 8, 1943—Convoy sailed along north of Sicily without incident until six in the evening when a German plane, an Fw-190, flew past our stern and starboard side and dropped two bombs. We fired our 40mm but missed. About seven o'clock, we sighted a huge place where debris was burning in the water. Evidently, a ship had gone down there. About nine at night, General Quarters was called, and flares were dropped all around.

Top: Seabees unloading trucks over a pontoon from an LST on one of the beaches at Salerno. Bottom: An LST unloading equipment and troops at one of the beaches at Salerno. Sights like this wrecked Spitfire were common on the beaches.

While we were preparing to land on the beaches of Salerno, Italy had already surrendered and an armistice strategically announced on September 8th. This would allow the Italian Navy time to move their ships to Allied harbors before the Germans could capture or destroy them.

At 1950 on September 8, with Italy's surrender now official, German Luftwaffe General Field Marshall Albert Kesselring ordered Operation ACHSE be executed. Operation ACHSE was the codename for the Germans disarming of the Italians after their surrender to the Allies. The Germans had been expecting Italy to surrender and had plans in place for the minute it occurred. They would take over the Italian coastal defensive positions quickly.

Meanwhile, our convoy continued heading for the beach at Salerno.

At about five in the morning, on September 9, 1943, I was still at General Quarters station and looking out to port when, all of a sudden, a large seagoing tug, anchored only 150 feet from our bow, seemed to rise out of the water. There was a huge ball of fire, and then it settled. I could hear the men on her cry for help and saw them running around on deck trying to put the fire out. [Most of the fire was put out, but the tug later sank.]

About this time, we launched our pontoons. An air raid came, and firing went on all around us. Bombs dropped, and shore guns fired at us. A smoke screen was laid down immediately. The USS *LST-386* proceeded to Green Beach and was being heavily shelled. Her pontoons were a mess of wreckage when she was forced to withdraw after sustaining much damage. [It was later disclosed that the USS *LST-386* hit a mine on the way to the beach. The explosion caused forty-three casualties.]

We were ordered into Green Beach also, but just before we hit, we were directed by radio to reverse our course since artillery fire was too great. At this time, German shells were landing all around us, and boy was everyone apprehensive! On our second try for the beach, it was the same story; the artillery fire was still too great, but with the use of smoke, we were able to get back out again. Our third attempt to beach was successful, and we hit the beach about two in the afternoon. Artillery was still firing at us, but we were lucky. The Army had its front line only eighty yards in front of our bow doors.

We could see everything. Soldiers crawled along a wall as if they were going to crawl into it. Across the field, Germans were using their 88s and machine guns. On the beach lay a wrecked airplane and many other wrecked vehicles. Some tanks were still burning. As I monitored the wheelhouse radio, I continued looking through the slits in the wheelhouse ports.

Smoke pots were put out on the beach to hide us from the Germans view. That hour on the beach was one of the most anxious hours of my life. The swish of the 88s shells remained in my ears for a long time.

The beach we landed our troops on was lost to the Germans that night but regained the next day. I often wonder what happened to all the troops and equipment we landed.

German war records have revealed that General Heinrich von Vietinghoff, commanding the German Tenth Army, had been expecting a landing in the Salerno Gulf for several days.

> On 7 September, when he [Vietinghoff] heard that large convoys were heading thither, the 16th Panzer Division and the Italian 222nd Coastal Division were already busy installing mine fields along the beaches, building strong points at the most likely landing places, digging tank traps, and preparing bridges for demolition.[10]

According to Morison, when the news of the Salerno landings reached the German Commander in the South of Italy (Kesselring), he confidently issued the following proclamation:

> The invading enemy in the area of Naples-Salerno and southwards, must be completely annihilated and in addition thrown from the sea. Only by so doing can we obtain change of the situation in the Italian area. I require ruthless employment of all might of the three army units. Every commanding officer must be aware of his historical responsibility. The British and Americans must realize that they are hopelessly lost against the concentrated German might. (War Diary German Naval Command Italy, 10 September 1943)[11]

From Radio Log USS *LST-388*

September 8, 1943

1801—Following sent from Malta Radio:

Armistice has been arranged between Italy and the Allies as from 1830 hours AAA Italian warship movements... (remainder of message too garbled)

September 9, 1943

0235—*LST-386* preceding to beach as scheduled

0256—Wave is on beach, believe all troops have embarked

0341—*LST-386* reports causeways gone

0422—*LST-386* urgent, we are under heavy bombardment—request fire support—fire is coming from beach dead ahead and to port thirty degrees.

0440—*LST-386* requests permission to retract—has not unloaded cargo, believe no danger of sinking—one engine disabled could not unload without causeway—we are being shelled request instructions.

0456—*LST-357* reports BT was unable to beach—gunfire was too heavy and had our range am hiding behind smoke screen over

0532—Green Beach about 900 yards right from where it was intended

0540—Bring *LST-388* on #9 of Green Beach—over

0545—All LSTs ordered to lay off Green Beach and wait fire support

0547—*LST-388* asks if she is to reverse course

0550—All reserve troops ordered to land on extreme right of Green Beach

0553—*LST-388* ordered to lay off until we see where you are at—lay off until we order you in to unload—over

0555—Green Beach requests more fire support

0557—Green Beachmaster sends following BT must have help in clearing artillery fire which is directed at LSTs landing at right flank of Green Beach—over

0602—Green Beachmaster sends BT that is very urgent—LST has been hit twice—over

0605—Green Beachmaster sends BT impossible to unload LSTs on Green Beach until artillery is wiped out—this is urgent—over

0616—Green Beachmaster sends BT must have help artillery fire inland cannot land LSTs on beach one on beach hit several times urgent—over

0725—*LST-386* being unloaded by LCT and requests smoke screen

0800—Green Beach will accept LSTs, but it is warned that artillery fire will be directed on them—over

0902—Green Beach has been re-established and has two unloading places—over—Green Beach has been re-established to right of silow and has two unloading places—a vertical green marker to right flank ready for unloading now—you are going too far to the right—over (above sent to *LST-388*)

0926—Green Beachmaster reports cannot operate Green Beach unless fire support is brought to knock out gun emplacements it is getting pretty hot—over

1000—Still need fire support on Green Beach—please hurry it along—we are pretty well dug in, so it is not very possible to move our position—over

1128—*LST-386* reports damage below water line

1237—Sent by *LST-388* BT—Have no smoke available—request smoke screen—over

1255—*LST-357* ordered in BT—come in at vertical green marker when *LST-388* has retracted—she will be unloaded in fifteen minutes

1323—There are to be no more LSTs loaded with vehicles for a while—there is congestion at the front, and there is no place to put vehicles until the infantry is penetrated further—over

1336—In as much as we cannot take LSTs, send in as many LCIs as you can to this beach—over

1336—*LST- 388* reports load off

1514—Where are these LCIs?—their need is very great

1535—Green Beach radio to be evacuated as there is no assurance of holding beach behind this area—am complying and will close set to open up later

1907—Red Alert

September 10, 1943

    0232—General Quarters Red Alert

    0345—Green Beach ordered to be re-established immediately by chief of staff—chief of staff said he ordered it established last night but has found it not established—entered return convoy

All along the Salerno coast, LSTs attempted to beach and unload their cargo under heavy gunfire. According to Morison, USS *LST-385* sustained three hits when coming into the beach, and two more when discharging her vehicles.

USS *LST-375*, approaching her designated beach at 0715, received two direct hits and more while unloading. These hits started fires and severed her elevator cable, preventing her from discharging her vehicles from the main deck. After a two-hour struggle, she moved out to the roadstead to try to repair the elevator. Again, she received a hit, which exploded below her bottom. (Despite her damage, the next day she managed to land her remaining vehicles and depart with a convoy that night.)[12]

USS *LST-336* beached when the front lines were only about 150 yards inland. For over an hour she was subjected to heavy fire from enemy shore batteries and suffered eleven direct hits. My ship, the USS *LST-388*, headed to the beach at the same time as the USS *LST-336*. Both were ordered to retreat because of heavy gunfire just before they were to hit the beach, but the USS *LST-336* had gone too far. I received the radio message giving the order that might have saved us a horrible fate. A radioman onboard the USS *LST-336* wrote a poem describing the situation entitled "One September Morn."

LST 388

One September Morn

I should like to tell a story
of a ship without a name.
There are many others like her,
but their numbers aren't the same.

T'is landing ships they call them,
cause they run upon the beach,
and drop their tanks and guns and trucks
where e're there's need for each.

Now this vessel I'm describing,
is by no means very small,
but when it came to giving names
they just numbered her that's all.

But I'm not so good at stories,
Oh, would that I could tell,
of smoke and fire and blood and guts,
on the day that she caught hell.

Oh God, I know not why I'm left,
so many died that day,
upon that beach, along the shore
of blue Salerno Bay.

T 'was a Netherlands destroyer,
how well I now recall,
that went in and laid a screen of smoke,
to hide the fleet from all.

Then thru this screen a vessel came
aheading for the shore,
and on her bow I'll n'er forget,
those numerals that she bore.

INVASION AT SALERNO

The batteries from the hills rang out,
  the shells tore through her mast,
her colors hit, her halyards sag,
  but she was coming fast.

The beach was Green, in name, that's all,
  the sands were running red,
the sky was filled with planes and shells,
  and Jerries spitting lead.

She hit that beach and lurched up far,
  amid those deafening roars,
her bow stood high upon the sands,
  as she opened wide her doors.

The ramp was quickly lowered,
  and out the brave did pour,
though many fell when they were hit,
  the rest went on for more.

Two hundred yards beyond the surf,
  a wall ran low and long.
T 'was here the German gunners lay,
  while mowing down our throng.

The vehicles came streaming out,
  within them men of steel,
the shells were falling closer now,
  and some were seen to reel.

The batteries numbering ten and eight,
  had missed with many a shell,
but now their target loomed up large,
  and they really rang the bell.

They tore her side with many holes,
  and the bow was belching flame,

her bridge was laid in ruins,
the control room was the same.

The decks were strewn with wounded,
among them lay the dead,
and down below they prayed to God,
and cared for those who bled.

Finally came the word "withdraw,"
the cargo was ashore,
this surely was a mighty task,
and they prayed as n'er before.

'Cause down below the waterline,
the sea came pouring in,
through gaping holes that were not seen
and made her hopes quite thin.

The engines roared, her screws churned up,
but the bow moved not an inch,
though engineers had worked like mad
destruction seemed a cinch.

And finally through the grace of God,
her bow began to sway,
t'was then they knew of miracles,
as she pulled out through the bay.

Though listing from her many wounds,
her colors still on high,
she headed back from whence she came,
and the crew all heaved a sigh.

It was many minutes later
that the Germans took the beach,
with tiger tanks and eighty eights,
but the ship was out of reach.

> She unloaded then her wounded
> on a ship that wore a cross.
> The dead were buried later,
> mid great sorrow o'er their loss.
>
> The ship and crew were yankee
> but the cargo put ashore,
> were gallant British soldiers,
> and their fighting days are o're.
>
> Now they call her "patches,"
> 'cause there was so much to fix
> but, to all who saw that battle
> she is known as three three six.
>
> —George F. Hall, Jr, RM 3/C USNR

According to Morison, the Luftwaffe made serious raids on the roadstead (at Salerno) using their new radio-controlled glide bombs. There were two types of radio controlled bombs: one with a range of about eight miles, speed 570 mph; the other had a range of three and one-half miles with a speed of 660 mph. Both were guided by radio from high-flying planes and carried a warhead explosive charge of 660 pounds.[13]

September 11, 1943—We are loading troops in Palermo, Sicily, for our second run to reinforce the beachhead at Salerno. Off the beachhead, the US cruiser USS *Savannah* was struck by a Fritz-X.

The Fritz-X was the first guided missile and the heaviest bomb ever to hit a United States Navy ship. The bomb went through three decks before exploding in the ammunition-handling room. The real target had been the control ship USS *Ancon*, Admiral Henry Kent Hewitt's flagship, on which was General Mark Clark. The USS *Savannah* survived the attack and was towed to Malta, but she never returned to combat. The British battleship HMS *Warspite* was also severely damaged by one of these new radio-controlled bombs and also had to be towed to Malta.[14]

September 14, 1943—Just before we reached the southern end of the beachhead at Salerno, General Quarters sounded, and another air attack occurred. I was out on deck when it began. A line of high-flying German planes peeled off and went into a dive. All guns opened up in an instant. Allied fighters could still be seen in the sky when this attack came. Just before we arrived in the bay, an American liberty ship had been hit and was still in flames.

We landed British troops again at Green Beach. After being ordered in at night, we were unloaded in about an hour. Immediately on completing unloading, we pulled out and anchored. All night, the sound of artillery could be heard in the hills, thrown by British destroyers on either side of us.

When we had beached, there was a British anti-aircraft crew set up within a few feet of the bow doors. They told some of the crew about the large number of casualties. The fields in back of the beach were littered with booby traps and land mines. A wounded British soldier said he thought the whole first wave was wiped out. They felt the Germans, somehow, had gotten hold of secret plans and maps of our invasion several days before we arrived.

The night before we arrived with this second load, the Germans drove almost to Green Beach. B-17 Flying Fortresses bombed them and were a major force in repulsing the counterattack.

While we were there, a large number of paratroopers were dropped onto the beach.

Much has been written about the invasion of Salerno since the war. Eric Norris, in his book *Salerno: A Military Fiasco*, states that September 13–14, 1943, were the critical days for the Allied forces on the beach. It appears that General Eisenhower and his commanders believed the timing of the Italian surrender would ease the invasion into "Fortress Europe."

The armistice, announced aboard ship prior to the landings, had indeed sounded like good news. At first the thoughts were on encountering Italian opposition on the beaches, which now would be minimal due to their surrender, but the Germans moved in quickly and were on the defense from the moment our convoys approached the beaches.

INVASION AT SALERNO

September 15, 1943—We are on our way south from Green Beach, heading to Palermo, Sicily. Artillery and tanks must be needed badly. Today's news stated that the Allies are slowly withdrawing. The British Eighth Army is coming up from the south of Italy and is only eighty miles away and advancing rapidly. We are all praying for the Fifth Army to hang in there.

The British Eighth Army, led by General Montgomery, quietly slipped across the Strait of Messina into the toe of the boot of Italy a few days prior to the landings at Salerno. The goal was to have German troops rush to the south in an effort to divert them from the real landing site, which was Salerno. Instead, Montgomery encountered very little resistance, and proceeded north, to meet up with the American Fifth Army at Salerno.

September 16, 1943—As we entered Palermo harbor, we passed twenty-two naval vessels, five of them submarines at anchor. All surrendered in good condition. This is the first we have seen of the Italian Navy since coming overseas.

Although devastated by bomb damage, Palermo reminds me of a US city. Granted a short liberty, we jumped at the chance for distraction by first riding all over town in a buggy. While walking down a street, an Italian civilian called out, "How are things going, Yanks?" It turned out he had lived in Brooklyn for several years. It was a pleasure to eat on the balcony of a fine restaurant which overlooked the main thoroughfare. First, we were served a large bottle of Italian wine, then spaghetti and lamb. The police stood out in their slick Napoleonic uniforms.

Our third trip back to Salerno proved uneventful. The Fifth Army didn't appear to have been able to enlarge the beachhead much. The loud sound of gunfire could still be heard from the hills. At night, large flashes lit up the sky, and naval vessels continued shelling the hills.

We made our way to Termini Imerese, a smaller port east of Palermo, to load more reinforcements, and then it was quickly back to the beaches of Salerno.

September 19, 1943—We have been to Termini Imerese, about eighteen nautical miles east of Palermo. The ship took on a cargo of large 155mm guns, ammunition, and troops. The fourth trip back to Salerno was routine sailing. Naval ships are still shelling inland.

As even more reinforcements and equipment were needed, we were diverted to other ports, such as the one at Tripoli, Libya, south of Tunisia.

September 24, 1943—We are on our way to Tripoli, Libya, a former Italian possession. We traveled through the Straits of Messina and passed Mount Etna, a volcano. The mountain was an impressive sight as the sun set. Only a short while ago, Mount Etna had been the scene of some bitter fighting.

September 26, 1943—We have arrived in Tripoli. A few hours before we got into port, there was a muster on the main deck. It was a beautiful day. The captain came out and gave a very touching talk. He complimented the crew for the way they handled themselves during the Sicilian and Salerno campaigns. The chief received a Purple Heart for getting a piece of shrapnel in his backside during an air raid. Others entitled to a Purple Heart are still in the hospital. We are all to receive a written letter of commendation.

Many Italian ships are sunk in Tripoli's harbor. The Italians must have spent millions to erect so many modern buildings here. The drive along the sea draws to mind an American seashore with many apartment buildings. Most of the town seems to be either Jewish or Arab with few Italians.

September 27, 1943—Today, we sailed from Tripoli for Salerno to deliver more troops and equipment. The crew would like to go back to Bizerte as all our clothes and seabags were left there when we went on the invasion. The trip back to Salerno was routine. With troops and equipment unloaded, we are now headed back to Tripoli.

October 7, 1943—We arrived in Tripoli again. I went ashore with Bob Lewis, and we unexpectedly found a nice restaurant. Good soup was served. There were plenty of vegetables but not much meat. No liquor was available. We ordered lemonade because of the limited choices. Later, in town, we paid one shilling for a thimble full of ice cream. It tasted funny and was probably made with goat's milk. Afterward, we bought some melons in the native market.

At six in the evening, the ship pulled out. We have suffered through British rations almost since leaving Bizerte. All Americans should be put on British rations from time to time so that they appreciate the quality of US rations! We are headed for the Italian naval base at Taranto, Italy.

October 8, 1943—We arrived in Taranto with our British soldiers and their equipment. Taranto had been a big Italian Navy operating base. The harbor is full of Italian naval vessels of all sizes.

Our short three-hour liberty made it impossible to get to see all of the port. The city is modern and, apparently, untouched with war damage. It seems we are among the first Americans to have liberty in Taranto. Often, we hear people exclaim "Americans" as we walk by them. Thousands of Italian sailors are on liberty in the town.

October 9, 1943—In the A.M., we proceeded through a narrow channel to the inner lake where the naval base is located. Thousands of people lined the street to watch as we passed through to the inner lake.

We tied up at a submarine shipbuilding yard to discharge. The large Italian liner, MS *Saturnia*, now a hospital ship, is anchored nearby.

The Americans seem to find the Italian naval personnel very friendly. I had liberty with an Italian-American fellow from Brooklyn. The moment he spoke to some Italian sailors in their own language, they got all excited. They insisted on taking us to an Italian NCO club and buying us wine. The Italians spent the night asking our friend from Brooklyn lots of questions.

October 10, 1943—We are on our way from Taranto to Bizerte. Soon we will get our mail, small stores, seabags, and replenish the ships low food supply.

October 15, 1943—We each received the following commendation:

U.S.S. LST 388

15, October 1943

    From: Commanding Officer
      To: von der Osten, Robert William 646 75 34 USNR
    Subject: Commendation

1. You are hereby commended this date at Captain's Meritorious mast for excellent performance of duty and displaying exceptional initiative in keeping with the highest traditions of the United States Navy during the initial assault invasions of both Sicily and Italy and the follow-up trips thereafter.

John A. Scott
Lieutenant USNR
Commanding

Round trips in the perilous waters between Africa, Sicily, and Salerno continued to fill most of our days and nights. For over a month we raced from port to beach, and beach to port, loading and unloading the needed reinforcements, guns, and equipment. German subs and E-boats, floating mines, and the Luftwaffe remained serious threats. Not only did we face these external threats, but also threats onboard our own ships. In addition to carrying troops, we also carried their guns, ammunition, and fully gassed vehicles. At times, we were sitting on a ship full of potential explosives. No doubt the soldiers aboard our ship thought about this as well.

Our experience at Salerno, had been, by far, the most terrifying of our experiences to date, and would remain so, with many of us I believe, for the rest of our lives.

Last Days in North Africa

B Y THE LATE FALL OF 1943, focus seemed to be shifting, at least for our ship. Although a new amphibious operation into Anzio, Italy was in the planning stages for January, the shift for us was to the UK, to prepare for the coming cross-channel attack into France. Before that happened, however, we had one last chance to visit the ancient city of Carthage.

October 25, 1943—Once back in Bizerte, we were granted liberty from ten in the morning to ten at night. It was well needed! Four of us hitched the sixty miles to the ancient ruins of Carthage. On the way, we rode in every type of army vehicle, from an ambulance to command car to truck. We saw the wreckage of German equipment that still dots the countryside for miles and miles on all sides of Tunis.

Although there were many camels, the Arabs seemed to prefer riding on the very rear end of burros. Some rode sideways and others rode on top of huge loads that almost covered the poor animal. Along the road huge cacti grew to nearly twice my height. Many were planted in rows surrounding fields. This is a good way to hide a watermelon patch. There are many vineyards here also.

The country surrounding Carthage is farmland. Everything is turning green and the farmers are starting to plow with their rough plows pulled by oxen. You can also see the oxen going round and round in a circle pulling a boom that helps pump water from a well.

I haven't read up on Carthage recently but from what I am told, it was a city of 700,000 population at the time it was destroyed by the Romans. It is more than 2,000 years old.

I can imagine the thrill the archeologists experienced when digging on what had been exposed so far. Most of the excavation has been done by Americans who started in 1905. One ruin pointed out by our guide was uncovered by the University of Michigan.

Upon arrival, we rented an old horse and buggy to ride around the ruins. Our first stop was at the arena where the gladiators fought. In the same arena prisoners were turned loose with lions. About this time the Arabs turned their children loose on us. Some of them had learned a smattering of English with some American slang. The kids tried to sell us alleged ancient Roman coins and pieces of pottery.

When we came up to the arena a little Arab came running up and showed us a note. It was supposed to be a recommendation, but instead read "This kid is no damn good as a guide. Do not hire him." We decided to hire a different guide, a little Arab who may have been about 15 years old. He took us around and gave a very colorful description of the things we saw.

As we stood on the ancient walls surrounding the arena, we could see cages of stone where the guards stayed in order to keep the prisoners from escaping. Down the center of the arena is a huge pit, with steps leading down. On one end is an enclosure where the lions were kept. On the opposite end is a small chapel. Most of this is original but some rebuilt in 1929. They say that Catholics make a pilgrimage to this spot each year. At right angles to the center of a runway is a tunnel that is under the floor of the arena. It leads to an enclosure where the prisoners were kept. Our guide imagined that the prisoners were fed with their hands tied spread-eagled to the wall. At times the lions were turned loose on them.

Parts of marble pillars still stand around the arena. The masons of that day must have been wonderful for the tunnels, guards cubicle, and walls were all of rock and clay.

When we were through looking around, our guide wanted payment. He wasn't satisfied with what we gave him. A cigarette sufficed for as long as it took to smoke, then he started hounding us again. We gave him a modest tip. We then ran the blockade of Arab children at the entrance and began looking for another guide.

One of several postcards obtained while on liberty touring the ancient city of Carthage. I wouldn't think of Carthage again for many years, until my young daughter Barbara invited me to see the movie *Patton* with her. Near the beginning of the movie you see the General, supposedly peering over the ruins of Carthage. It brought back a lot of memories.

We next decided to explore a Roman Catholic Church on top of the hill. It had been started in 1884. It is of Arabic architecture, and is beautiful and colorful. There are many Arabic designs of small squares put together. We found ourselves whispering in the church without realizing it.

Afterwards, we made our way to the museum. The rediscovering of Carthage is carried on by the Roman Catholics and is in the hands of the great white fathers. No guide is allowed in the museum for good reason. A lot of the guides are Arabs who are noted thieves. There is a sign on the gate which states. "No Allied troops allowed." Some officers rang the gate bell and went in. We just followed them inside.

The museum is a fairly large building, with a large patio in the center. The work of diffing is still going on under the supervision of priests. All other work has been stopped for the duration as most of it has been carried on by Americans.

The first thing that catches your eye is a small chapel in the center of the patio with a small, ancient, white marble cross sticking up in the center. A priest paced up and down a short foot path. He had a small pointed beard and, as he walked back and forth slowly, his black gown gave him a stately but mysterious look. He was reading a small bible from which he never glanced up or looked to either side. The priest seemed to have a wonderful power of concentration.

There were all kinds of artifacts from the ancient city. All the marble was brought over from Italy over 2,000 years ago. There was lots of it.

When we left the museum, we finally found an English speaking guide. He was in his late teens, an Italian who had emigrated from the island of Pantelleria. The hansom cab (a kind of horse-drawn carriage) we went around in was driven by a Frenchman. The cost of the horse drawn vehicle was 300 francs ($6.00). A rip off.

This new guide took us to the Roman ruins. All that is left to see are some walls of buildings and huge floors of public buildings that still showed tiles in intricate designs and of different colors. The guide pointed out the grain storage bins, and the system of collecting and storing water. Down near the ocean you could see the reservoir for the city's water. I don't know if this is where the huge aqueduct empties though. This stone Roman aqueduct runs for 80 miles inland. At places, it is 100 feet high.

Our guide also pointed out where the present Bey of Tunis (their monarch) lives overlooking the sea. The view from the ruins looks over the blue Mediterranean.

We came to a large villa that was so big that it must have belonged to some Roman senator or administrator. The pillars are still perfect.

The old Roman theatre was our next stop. It has an average sized stage with an orchestra pit in front with marble seats. I understand Churchill spoke from this stage a few months ago.

It was then time to pay our guide. He let us name our own price. I added a package of American cigarettes which he seemed to appreciate. The Arab children were still around and trying to sell us old coins.

The sun was sinking fast as we left to catch a cold, windy ride back to the ship. We arrived back cold, wet, tired and hungry for we hadn't eaten since breakfast. Yet, it had all been worth it.

October 26, 1943—We have been at Bizerte for quite a while, undergoing engine and general repairs performed by ship's company [crew]. Pontoons have been put back on our sides. These pontoons are welded, which probably means a long trip. The rumor is that we are going to England.

I met hometown friend Jack Horan who is still communications officer on USS *LST-355*. His ship has been changed to an anti-aircraft LST, with 20mm and 40mm guns all over it. There is nothing like meeting an old friend from home after being overseas so long. We had some cake and coffee before he sent his small boat back to the USS *LST-388* with me.

November 10, 1943—We sailed from Bizerte for the last time and headed for Oran in Algeria. Outside the harbor, we took a disabled LCT [landing craft, tank] in tow. The radio room seemed rather nice after standing so many visual watches the past month.

November 14, 1943—Because of bad weather, we put into the port of Mostaganem, Algeria, with our disabled LCT. The rest of the convoy continued on to their destination. We had quite a time getting tied up. Lines and cables kept breaking as the ship banged against the jetty. We now have a big dent in our starboard bow.

November 15, 1943—A shipmate, Mac, and I went on liberty in the old port of Mostaganem. We got a ride in a truck from the dockyard, up the long hill to the city. There are fewer soldiers here now. At a native market, we got into a dispute with an Arab and refused to buy the oranges he wanted to sell. At a bar, we had a good time drinking beer, singing, and joking, but the Algerian beer doesn't compare with American brands. We stopped and watched a funeral go by. The coffin was drawn in a wagon-hearse and decked in black velvet. All the family and friends of the deceased walked behind.

We hired a taxi to take us back to the ship. On reaching the gate, we had another dispute, this time with the cab driver who tried to overcharge us.

When I returned to the ship, I was selected to stand the 8:00 p.m. to midnight watch. I finished John Steinbeck's book *The Grapes of Wrath* while on watch.

November 17, 1943—We sailed for Oran with our LCT in tow, arriving at our destination without incident.

While in Oran, we had LCT-305 placed on the top deck and an LCM [landing craft mechanized] placed inside it. An extension was put on the conning tower [raised platform from which an officer gives directions] so that it would be easier to see over the LCT.

When we had liberty, we went to a place in Oran called the Waldorf. It was like a nightclub in the States—modernistic, low blue lights, and a small stage. The native orchestra played American songs, and only American soldiers and sailors were allowed inside. Every once in a while, a soldier came up and played one of the instruments. The Red Cross Empire was another hangout for most of the crew. It was a big theater.

Also, while in Oran, we celebrated our ship's birthday by having an extra-good feed and pictures taken of the crew. [The USS LST-388 had been commissioned Nov. 20, 1942.] We would also spend Thanksgiving there.

November 24, 1943—It's Thanksgiving. Someone broke into the refrigerator and stole the ice cream that was to be the crews' holiday treat. We haven't had ice cream in months. Lt. Meehan, the executive officer, got so angry that he canceled liberty. He is an old Navy bos'n mate in peacetime and can be very nasty. Meehan has never liked me, and I have never liked him. We were all ordered to bring our hammocks to the main deck and were required to scrub them under the hot sun. [No one ever admitted to the theft of the ice cream.]

Lt. Meehan was rough on the deck crew but, in short order, made good sailors out of them. Everything had to be shipshape all the time. He just didn't fit with the other officers who were reserves. When we arrived in England, Meehan had a girlfriend waiting for

While in Oran, Algeria, in the fall of 1943, we had a crew photo taken. I am on the first row, fifth sailor over, from the left. Our ship, USS *LST-388*, was now officially one year old as it had been commissioned back in November of 1942 in Norfolk, VA.

him. I don't know what she saw in ugly old Meehan. She just happened to be at the pier, waving to her beloved as we docked. While there, Lt. Meehan was transferred and given his own command. Good riddance.

The reserve officers on our ship were a pretty good bunch. They stretched the rules once in a while but nothing serious. A number of times, girls were brought aboard and wined and dined in the officers' wardroom. Enlisted men were never permitted the privilege of female company onboard.

One time, just after we got underway, my communication officer had the conn. I was on the conning tower with the signalman acting as recorder for his light messages. The officer had been drinking before we got underway, and the liquor must have gotten to him when the ship began to roll. He got so sick and just laid down on the deck. We let him lay there awhile because the captain had secured for the night. The signalman conned the ship, and no one knew the difference.

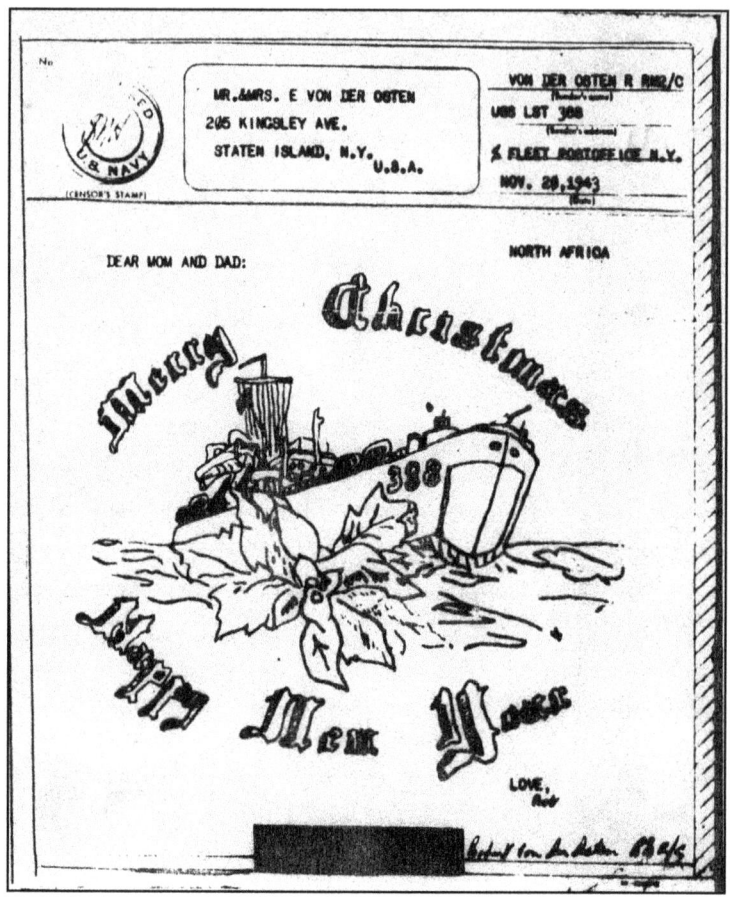

Whenever possible, I liked sending v-mail (Victory Mail), like this, home to my family. This one is from North Africa to my parents in New York.

The officers were friendly enough aboard ship but never socialized with the men ashore. Onboard, the officers' quarters were off limits to enlisted personnel.

Our days in the Mediterranean were winding down. LSTs and the smaller landing craft had proved themselves as formidable tools in amphibious assaults, first at Sicily and then at Salerno. Winston Churchill, with regard to this period of the war in Italy, had this to say:

In this period in the war, all the great strategic combinations of the Western Powers were restricted and distorted by the shortage of tank landing-craft for the transport, not so much of tanks, but of vehicles of all kinds. The letters L.S.T. (Landing Ship, Tanks) are burnt in upon the minds of all those who dealt with military affairs in this period.[15]

December 1, 1943—We are sailing from Oran for what we believe is somewhere in England. Africa and Italy will remain but a memory.

Voyage to England

LEAVING BEHIND AFRICA and the Mediterranean, I thought we would put in at Gibraltar, but our ship passed right by. We sailed through the strait on the African side and Gibraltar could be seen about ten miles away. Large schools of porpoise surrounded us all day.

December 4, 1943—It has been showery all day. The Atlantic is getting rough, and the ship takes an awful beating when she buries her bow deep into the waves. She shakes from stem to stern. At times, spray goes clear over the conning tower. Many of our Seabees are seasick. Sleeping in the crews' quarters is next to impossible; the fantail bounces up and down, like a springboard. The ship continues to roll violently, but I do not feel even a bit sick. I ate a fairly good meal. The crew seems to be abnormally quiet.

We're experiencing a little trouble with the radio equipment. My ignorance as to troubleshooting and repair annoys me, but I think one of the aerials is faulty. Tonight, at eight-forty, General Quarters rang, and a plane dropped flares astern of us. Nothing further developed. We are on the starboard side of a large merchant convoy. All day, we have been heading west.

December 5, 1943—It is not quite as rough as yesterday, but sleeping still proves difficult. We are somewhere off the coast of Portugal on course 293. Another section from Casablanca [Morocco] joined the convoy making this the biggest convoy outside of the invasions that I have ever been in. Casablanca's radios come in very strong.

December 8, 1943—It was extremely rough last night, so I slept very little. The ship shook so violently during the early hours of the A.M. that some fellows were thrown from their bunks. The seas are really mountainous. One minute the ships in the convoy are way above us, and the next minute we are above them. When the bow buries into a big wave, the ship seems to stop dead with its screws [propellers] out of the water, turning madly. The vibration is such that a few plates across the main deck have cracked. Our course is dead north.

I had an interesting talk with one of the members of the new, small-boat crew. This fellow was in the initial invasion of North Africa where LSTs were not used. The invasion fleet was eleven transports and small boats. The fighting with the Germans and the Vichy French was heavier than most people were led to believe. The organization of the small boats into groups of six did not go smoothly, but they did an excellent job.

Casablanca was shelled from fifteen miles out. A few days later, this sailor got into Casablanca and saw the heavy damage to the city. The sight of the French battleship FS *Jean Bart* and the smaller naval craft was eye-opening. The entire invasion, from the time he left the States until his return, took only a month and a half. He told me of the sinking of the transport *Scott*. My boot camp friend, Bill Vesely, was on her. It seems the French people are not all that unhappy with the Germans after the defeat of France.

December 10, 1943—For the last two days, we have had smooth sailing. We are about 500 miles from the nearest land, heading north. There was a warning from our escorts that we had been sighted by German planes. I went up the mast and fixed the faulty aerial. It sure gave me a thrill and a little fear when walking out onto the cable with yardarm in hand while the ship rocked. Those old-time sailors on the clipper ships sure were brave fellows.

December 11, 1943—Today was smooth sailing, but fog hung over the sea all day. We are still headed north. President Roosevelt is touring the Mediterranean, Malta, Cape Bon, Tripoli [Libya], and El-Alemein [Egypt]. I am reading Wendell Willkie's book *One World*.

I would like to see Willkie win the presidency (if he were to run again). Roosevelt has done a good job, but it is time for a change.

December 12, 1943—We are almost to the coast of Ireland. It is rumored our destination is Londonderry, Northern Ireland. At five-twenty this afternoon, General Quarters was sounded as a submarine had been detected by the escorts. The convoy began to zigzag its course and split in all directions. Nothing happened.

December 13, 1943—This was the worst day of the voyage. We plowed through some of the biggest waves I have ever seen. It is feared that the pontoons on the starboard side may be carried away if the weather does not moderate. They are starting to break loose from their weldings. An extra big wave hit us broadside and shook up the entire ship.

December 14, 1943—Today, via blinker, I found out that our real destination is to be Plymouth, England. There has never been a trip in which our destination was kept so in the dark. We are now sailing near the north coast of Ireland. The entire convoy has its running lights on, and it looks like a city lit up on our port side.

December 15, 1943—Today, we rounded the north coast of Ireland. The weather is clear, the seas calm, but the air is cold. Fresh water on board is in short supply, so showers and washing of clothes are prohibited. We have left the large convoy and have been routed south through the Irish Sea.

December 16, 1943—After proceeding south all day, we are off the south coast of England. I received two SOS calls on my watch last night from ships being shelled by submarines.

December 17, 1943—We have arrived in Milford Haven, Wales. There are quite a few ships anchored around us. There are also a few sunken ships nearby. Our anchorage is at the mouth of a river, and we have not had a view of the town.

December 20, 1943—We arrived at Plymouth, England this morning. It is a large port. This afternoon I was on a food-securing party, and we got off the small boat at the wrong place on purpose so we could walk through town. Our working party stopped at two pubs where good beer was served. It was a treat to go into a clean place where English is spoken. The people seemed most friendly.

When we got to the USS *LST-5*, our supplies were not of American origin but British rations. The boys were disappointed as British stores are inferior to ours. I was responsible for letting 150 lbs. of Argentine beef fall into the water; the knot I tied didn't hold. We retrieved it with a boat hook. We had a great many loaves of bread that were forced on us. The fellows were really sinful the way they treated that food. Much of it was discarded. The way the crew treated that bread made me realize how spoiled we Americans are.

December 22, 1943—Had my first liberty in England. After stopping at an English pub in Davenport, we took a double-decker bus into Plymouth. We passed blocks and blocks of burned-out buildings. In the center of the city, about seventy-five percent of the buildings are in ruins.

I heard we could send cables home, so I went to the Red Cross and sent one home. "Merry Christmas and Happy New Year—Well and safe in England." The Red Cross building had a cafeteria, rooms for the night, a game room, and a reading room.

We went to a restaurant in town and had chicken. While there, I became friendly with an English sailor. He is married and lives in Ipswich. Since his home was blitzed, his family took over a large farm. He showed us pictures of the beautiful place. I hope to visit it sometime. He warned me to bring a ration card and train priority. Our new friend showed us about town, and then he had to go back. We then went to see the movie, *Alexander's Rag Time Band*.

At the theater, I talked to a sweet Irish girl who was on an ack-ack [anti-aircraft] crew. Could have taken her out, but there wasn't enough time. When we got outside, the city was blacked out. Boy, was it dark! (Remember, we are only ninety-five miles across the channel from France.) Two of the fellows from our ship were shining their flashlights on the way to the liberty boat, and some young

VOYAGE TO ENGLAND

During my first liberty after arriving in Plymouth, England, I sent this telegram home to my mother, letting her know I was well and safe, and in England.

girls yelled to put out that torch. We started talking to them and found out they were on the way to work on the night shift. I discovered that the one I was talking to had a piece of mistletoe on her coat. I said I bet she couldn't put it over her head. Much to my delight, she did, so I kissed her. When we got back to the ship, I had a slew of letters. A wonderful Christmas present!

December 23, 1943—We pulled out today for Portsmouth. The sea is calm and the weather cloudy.

December 24, 1943—About 2:00 A.M., the general alarm went off and nearly knocked me out of the sack. I rushed to my station, and there were flares all about. Gunfire and tracers sailed up in the air and along the water everywhere. This kept up all around us for two and a half hours. We were ordered to an anchorage and had to wait until the morning to proceed. Besides planes, German E-boats also attacked us. It was an odd feeling to see those tracers bounce off the water.

We listened to a German news broadcast describe the action. They said a formation of E-boats attacked a convoy in the channel and were aided by flares dropped from planes. Their claims of damage were ridiculous.

General Dwight D. Eisenhower has been named Supreme Commander of the Invasion Forces.

December 25, 1943—Pulled into Portsmouth this A.M. Some fellows got twenty-four-hour liberty, but mine doesn't come up until the 27th. We had a very nice Christmas dinner. The invasion is rumored to be scheduled within the next ninety days. The American people are being warned to prepare for a casualty list of 500,000.

The Long Wait

OUR ARRIVAL IN ENGLAND, in late 1943, proved uplifting for our crew, even though we had no idea exactly when the next invasion would take place. As it turned out, we had a long wait, just over five months, until the invasion at Normandy in France. We spent these months in various ports of the United Kingdom, including those of England, Wales, and Northern Ireland. More training, practice invasions, ship maintenance and repair, and, of course, memorable liberties, filled those months. Fortunately, I was again able to make the best of my granted time off, temporarily getting away from the intensity of the war and away from the cramped confines of the ship. It started with a twenty-four-hour liberty in London.

London

December 27, 1943—I got my twenty-four-hour liberty and went to London with several others. What a time! After buying a railroad ticket, there was about an hour to wait. Nearby, we met three nice-looking girls at a pub. They insisted on seeing us off to the train. The train ride lasted an hour and a half and went through a good deal of the countryside. It reminded me of certain parts of Pennsylvania or New England.

Once in London, we took the Underground [subway] into the heart of the city. Some of the fellows picked up girls [called commandos] without delay. We did a little sightseeing, and then booked a room in a real nice hotel. There were fluffy blankets, soft mattresses, and a radio.

We ate at a very nice Red Cross Club and later managed to get into a pub. I started talking with a free Pole who had been held prisoner by the Germans for a year and then managed to escape. His method was most novel. He changed his name and obtained a false passport and papers, then pretended to be a regular civilian. He went through the Balkans and managed to get to a British ship which sailed to Egypt. He is now in England, going to radio school. He likes scotch and drinks it like water.

I enjoyed going to a dance at Covent Gardens. In peacetime, it is the home of the London Opera. The setting is like dancing in a huge, king's court, and there are about three girls to every man. Only a handful of Americans were among the thousands of dancers. There was a big, marvelous dance floor, and two large orchestras switched every hour. A huge crystal ball hung high up in the center, and a spotlight flashed on it. At times, the music was soft, and the house lights went low, and just spotlights revolved around and around. I met a real swell girl and we stuck together most of the evening.

A British Air Force man and I left the dance at the same time and managed to meet two real nice looking girls. We took them to a night club and had a few drinks. I found the one I was with to be some bundle of charms. Afterwards we walked through the pitch black, blackout to the train station so the girls could catch their train.

Back at the hotel, I found the snack bar still opened. There I met two new fellows from my ship and a soldier. We talked and had a few drinks before I excused myself, as it was quite late. When I got into the swell bed, I found myself in dreamland immediately! I didn't even hear the next fellow (three of us had taken a room together) come in. My buddy said he came in fifteen minutes after me. It was great to sleep in a nice, soft bed for a change.

On the train returning to Portsmouth, everyone reported having a good time. What stories they had to tell!

December 31, 1943—We left Portsmouth with the LCT-305 in tow. Our next port of call is Weymouth, England. It is said that we are the first American sailors to come ashore in this port for years. [They were to see a lot more Americans in the near future.] This is New Year's Eve, and at least, I got off the ship for a little while. Last New Year's Eve, I spent aboard ship.

We had been overseas almost a year by now. So much had happened in that year and none of us were the same men as we were when we first joined the navy. How could we be.

January 7, 1944—We are moored to a buoy in Plymouth harbor. I had liberty today. When entering a restaurant, I ran across my hometown friend, Lt. Jack Horan. He has been transferred to an admiral's staff. I told him how our ship has changed groups, and our pay accounts are all messed up. He wanted to lend me some money. We have drained the canteen fund and have borrowed from the Red Cross.

The ship is being painted, and all we seem to do is paint and chip, chip and paint.

In mid-January, while still in Plymouth, we were granted a five-day leave. This was the most free time I had had in two years. I decided I would see as much of London as possible.

January 13, 1944—The USS *LST-388* is moored to a buoy off Davenport [Plymouth], and our small boat took us ashore, where we walked in a drizzle to the railroad station. Heavy Blitz damage lay all around us. I wired the Strand Palace Hotel in London to reserve a room, and I also sent a wire to the girl I met on my first trip here.

Three of us boarded the train and found an empty compartment. Our fellow travelers in the compartment seemed to change at every stop. The last four passengers were American soldiers, replacements awaiting assignment to a unit. It was a pleasant ride through the beautiful English countryside. At Exeter, we had beer and some poor sandwiches. The English passengers smartly brought their lunch. We pulled into Waterloo Station just at twilight.

It was a short walk from the station to the Strand Palace Hotel. After a brief wait, I was given a room. I met a soldier while in the lobby, and he and I had dinner in the grill. Later, we went to the dance at Covent Gardens. The girl I wired never showed. Just as well, for soon, I met a swell girl named Muriel Mountford. We danced and talked the night away. She let her girlfriend go home without her. There was an underground station outside the dance, but we ignored it and walked to the next one. On leaving her at her home, she promised to meet me Saturday in the lobby of my hotel. I returned to the Strand Palace, and the soft bed was wonderful.

January 14, 1944—After breakfast, I went with three shipmates and had individual pictures taken. They were small and expensive (over a pound for two). I had one sent to mom and the other sent to me on the ship. A character at the studio said to me, "You can blame the war on yourselves for you waited so long to get into it." He saved himself by adding "You have done a darn good job for the time you have been in it." We walked through Lester Square and proceeded to get lost.

My shipmates, Snead and Auck, had to take a nap after lunch. (Can't tell you why they were so tired as ladies might read this.) While they slept, I visited the Red Cross Rainbow Club. As I walked through the door, the desk clerk called, "One person, wanted to go sightseeing in a cab." I quickly volunteered. The cab left with four of us sailors.

Our cabby was quite intelligent and never stopped talking. We went down Piccadilly through the worst bombed out parts of the city. He told us how long they burned and described the actions of the people during the Blitz. We went into St. Paul's Cathedral. Its dome is much like the capitol's in Washington, and it has a whispering balcony. The cabby told us the history of the church. One bomb had entered the building but did not explode. Buildings for blocks around were devastated.

On passing the Tower of London, the cabby gave another history lesson from the time of Edward VIII, who beheaded his wives, until the internment of Rudolph Hess [deputy to Adolph Hitler].

Westminster Abby wasn't as big as I expected. At one time, the cabby said I was standing on the head of Ben Jonson [English playwright and poet]. He is the only man buried there standing up. Another time, the cabby claimed I was standing on the feet of Thomas Hardy [English novelist and poet]. When we came to the Statue of [Edward] Cornwallis [lieutenant in the Revolutionary War] he remarked, "He was a great, man but I am afraid Mr. [George] Washington caught him napping once." We also saw the House of Commons and Big Ben.

In the evening, Auck and I visited the Paramount Dance Hall, which fellows on the ship raved about. I saw some of the craziest jitterbugging imaginable.

January 15, 1944—I met Muriel in the lobby about noon. She looked very lovely and showed her friendly smile. Snead and a girl he met in the grill queue [line] had lunch with us. The lunch was hardly passable for there is a shortage of almost everything. Seems strange how these English eat almost everything with spoon and fork. After the meal, we walked to Lester Square and saw the movie, *Jane Eyre*. A good organist played at intermission. Later, we had dinner in the grill and listened to the orchestra. I couldn't stop looking at Muriel across the table. She has such a lovely smile. Her eyes sparkle.

After supper, Muriel and I walked and talked. An air raid siren went off, and we could hear gunfire in the distance, but soon, the all-clear sounded. I kissed her several times on the way back. We made the last train to her home. She insisted I go to her house the next day and meet her parents.

January 16, 1944—A friend was having my uniform cleaned and brought it back just in the nick of time. I met Muriel, and we took a cab to Westminster Abby where the choir was singing. The service was held in the Poet's Corner. After church, we strolled through the Cloisters, visited St. Margaret's Church as well as Westminster Cathedral. Our walk passed Parliament and crossed over the Westminster Bridge.

After not too long a ride on the underground, we arrived at Muriel's home. Her lovely parents had an open fire going in the fireplace. Mr. and Mrs. Mountford were very hospitable. He was reading a book, *The End of Africa*. When I went into the dining room, I was astonished at the wonderful meal Muriel's mother had set out. She must have spent hours preparing it and used half of their ration books. I felt very guilty. It was the best meal I have had since leaving home. Mrs. Mountford apologized for her war cooking. After dinner, we talked, listened to the wireless [radio], and heard Muriel play the piano. She played several pieces my brother Herb played at home. Then, Mrs. Mountford brought in several kinds of pie and tea. At the train station, I kissed Muriel goodbye and promised to write often. She promised to send me her picture. I hated to leave her.

When I got to Lester Square, the fog was thicker than ever. It was so black that I couldn't see a person standing just alongside me. My torch [flashlight] had burned out. I was like a blind man groping in the dark. Every once in a while, someone came near me with a light, and I asked them for directions to the Strand Hotel. It was a relief when an Englishman took me in tow and led me to the hotel.

January 17, 1944—I got up late. After breakfast, I wrote a note to Muriel. I bought a gift and took it to Muriel's mother. I had fifteen minutes to spare when I finally arrived at Waterloo Station. I had a window seat which gave me a marvelous view of the countryside. An English soldier filled the vacant seat in our compartment. We could not buy food on the train, so the soldier insisted we share his lunch. A lady came into the compartment later and insisted I share one of her sandwiches. At a large station, I managed to get some buns, tea, and magazines to share. This helped me reciprocate my fellow passengers' kindness. On arriving in Davenport, we were informed the ship had sailed. We had to spend the night at the Red Cross.

January 18, 1944—A boat taking orders to the USS *LST-388* gave us a lift to the ship. There was quite a bit of mail waiting. One letter was from Barbara Bryant, the girl I had cabled to meet me in London who never showed. She claimed she had the flu. The next time we met, she said she had intended to tell me she was married. Women? I gained by meeting Muriel.

January 23, 1944—I am twenty-four today. We are still in Davenport. As soon as the weather permits, we will sail for Falmouth.

They really are getting strict onboard. The ship is becoming all regulation. Reveille is at six fifteen, and we must be on the tank deck for exercises at six thirty. There was a captain's inspection again yesterday. Bunk and locker inspections take place regularly. Unless we do extremely dirty work, undress blues [work clothes] are the uniform of the day. There was a heavy air raid on London yesterday.

January 31, 1944—Still at Davenport, working hard to keep everything shipshape.

There were times when our ship needed to go into dry dock for maintenance or repair. It had proved quite the workhorse while in the Mediterranean, and, no doubt would become one again once the invasion into France took place. The ship had to be ready, whenever the time came. And it had to be ready for the training for the invasion, which began in force starting in February.

February 11, 1944—We have been in a big, grave dry dock at the Plymouth navy yard for four days. I was working on the bridge tarpaulin when I heard someone yelling down at the bottom of the grave [dry] dock for a stretcher. When I looked over the side, there lay one of the deck crew. He had been painting the side of the ship when a line holding his seat, attached to a rail stanchion, gave way when a weld broke loose. He fell twenty feet or more onto the stone dock bottom. I ran down and got a pharmacist mate and the stretcher. We obtained a heaving line and lowered it to those below. The sailor was badly hurt.

February 12, 1944—This morning, we left Plymouth and arrived in Dartmouth without incident. It is a beautiful town at the mouth of the Dart River. Our group is scheduled to go on a mock invasion, so no shore leave has been granted.

Dartmouth became an advanced amphibious base, with its main function being the servicing and repairing of landing ships and smaller landing craft. Its location also became a prime spot for practicing invasions.

February 15, 1944—We pulled into an earthen hard along the river and took on troops and equipment last night. This A.M., we left on our practice invasion. A lot of work goes into these mock runs. After sailing at night, we reached a location where the cruisers bombarded the coast. Rocket ships [converted LCTs] shot their charges off, and tanks fired from the LCTs. We had a walkie-talkie, and I had to stand continuous watch on the conning tower with it. We did not beach because of excessive tides. Some LSTs unloaded onto LCTs, and others onto pontoon barges propelled by huge outboard motors. The unloading was a slow go. Troops went over the side on nets into LCVPs [landing craft, vehicle and personnel]. This constituted the first wave. We returned to Dartmouth very tired.

I had liberty in this beautiful little town. We saw a movie then had some beans and chips, after which we went to a dance. At the dance, I met a very nice WRNS [Women's Royal Navy Service, popularly known as Wrens, equivalent to the US Navy WAVES, Women Accepted for Volunteer Emergency Service]. I hope to see her tomorrow night.

I gossiped, by blinker and semaphore, with the Wrens who manned the signal tower ashore, before we shifted anchorage. They didn't look bad through the glasses.

Orphans as Guests

Our next port of call would be the small, cozy fishing village of Brixham. Piers and a ramp had recently been built on the breakwater to accommodate all the bigger ships coming in and out of its port. It was also home to the British Seaman's Boys Home, a home for the orphan sons of deceased British seamen, founded in 1863.

February 23, 1944—We have been in Brixham Harbor for over a week. Every day, we participate in maneuvers. Liberty isn't much.

February 27, 1944—We are still at Brixham, participating in daily maneuvers.

Yesterday, the captain invited a group of little orphan boys from a seaman's orphanage to come aboard for evening chow. They were all about seven or younger and dressed in British sailor uniforms. It didn't take them long to be all over the ship, from the conning tower, radio room, officers' quarters, to the ramp room.

This supposedly tough crew of the USS *LST-388* didn't take long to soften up; the real tough guys seemed to have the most fun with the kids. The crew stocked them up with candy and books, and several, especially shipmate Fernandez, played music for them.

We had half the crew searching for two that got lost, but they were found in the main control room. One of the kids had lost a hatband, and they were looking for it.

Pictures were taken of all our little guests. They all marched down the pier in formation with their arms swinging smartly. I understand they are very strict with the orphans at the home. All the little boys wanted to join the Navy and visit Yankee land. On leaving, they had to pass up a high hill near the ship and kept waving and yelling back.

Stratford-upon-Avon

Around *March 10, 1944*, we were lucky enough to be granted a forty-eight-hour leave. A shipmate and I decided to make a dash for Stratford-upon-Avon, birth and burial place of William Shakespeare, some distance away. We arrived by train quite late, and a nice British couple showed us to the William and Mary Hotel, built in the seventeenth century.

After securing a charming room in this picturesque old inn, we made a dash for the rustic, old pub called the Windmill. Ten o'clock was the pub closing time. Civilians told us that they had seen many American soldiers, but we were the first American sailors to be in town for a long time.

The Red Cross had taken over the Old White Swan Hotel and had tours, which used Army trucks, leaving from the hotel. We made the two o'clock tour. There were ten in our party, all soldiers but us. We visited Shakespeare's house, Harvard House, Nash's House,

Trinity Church, Shakespeare Memorial Theatre, Anne Hathaway's [Shakespeare's wife] cottage, and several other places. When the tour ended, we just had time to eat in the Shakespeare restaurant before rushing for the train. We had to travel all night to get back to the ship on time.

I never went on liberty with this shipmate again. He was too lazy to walk to the end of the hall in the hotel to go to the bathroom. There was a sink in our room, so he urinated in it and then ran the water. I didn't care for this.

March 25, 1944—We are outward bound from Plymouth, England, and heading for Londonderry, Northern Ireland.

In April 1944, beaching craft, including the USS *LST-388*, received important alterations. These included new radio installations and bow door modifications. LSTs were also fitted with considerably more antiaircraft artillery.[16]

With the addition of new guns on our ship, gunnery practice increased. The target would be a sleeve towed by an aircraft. Preparations for the Normandy invasion, on a large scale, were in progress. Still, the date and time of the invasion remained unknown to us.

April 25, 1944—It has been a month since I got around to writing. We arrived in Londonderry safely after penetrating a very heavy fog. A submarine popped up in front of us just before entering the Londonderry channel. It gave us all an anxious moment until the recognition signals were flashed. The approach to Londonderry affords one a beautiful panorama, including a view of ruins of an old castle.

Just outside the city, we unloaded all our ammunition. It was an all-hands job. I felt the hard labor for several days. At Londonderry, no time was wasted in fitting the ship with extra guns. While there, a fellow working on the ammunition lockers told me of an old neighbor of mine from Staten Island, Dr. Amoury, who was a doctor on the base.

THE LONG WAIT

The part of the town we saw was a bit disappointing. It looked so beautiful from a distance. There was plenty of Irish whiskey to be had, and girls were easy to get at a price. Three of us were walking down a street when a buxom lass leaned out a second story window and offered us a good time at a reasonable price. One of the fellows took her up on her proposal. We waited outside for him. It didn't take very long, and he came out of the building bleary-eyed. I would have liked to have followed him, for the girl sure was enticing, but I just couldn't make myself do it.

In the evening, we went to a dance at Corinthian Hall. The first girl I danced with asked me if I was Protestant or Catholic. As usual, in the end, I found an exceptionally nice girl to spend time with. Too bad I couldn't see her again before the ship pulled out.

The following day, I got to see Dr. Amoury. He was busy, but soon, he asked me to come to his room. The room was one end of a Quonset hut. We had a beer together, talked about his family and our overseas experiences. His time was limited, but I was glad he saw me. I will have to write his daughter, Gloria, of our meeting.

From Londonderry, we went to Milford Haven, Wales. The new guns, 20mm and 40mm, more than double our firepower. We are proud of them.

While at Milford Haven, ten of us went to church in town, and the preacher spoke of willpower. He told the old story of Bobby Burns who tried to stop drinking. One day, after much effort, Bobby passed the last pub on the way home. He felt so proud of himself for having the willpower to pass the pub that he thought he deserved a reward. He rewarded himself by going back for one glass of ale.

At Milford Haven, thirteen men were transferred to the States. We then sailed for Cardiff, Wales, and the ship docked at Penarth. It took about twenty minutes by train to get to the center of Cardiff.

We have taken on twenty pharmacist mates. They will be with us until after the invasion. One of them named Kearn comes from Innis Street in Staten Island, my hometown.

During that sail to Penarth, we had some anxious moments when our ship engines stopped due to water in the fuel, leaving us in what was referred to as "out of control" status. Fortunately, we drifted with the current, maintaining our course, and the wind kept us where we needed to be. Another LST in the convoy, USS *LST-356*, took us in tow. The tow line snapped but fortunately, by that time, our engines could be started again. We rejoined the convoy as before with no additional problems.

Once at Penarth, training continued to intensify. Aircraft identification, chemical warfare, fire and damage control, signal training, and more firing practice. Army personnel came aboard to install tank deck tracks, and an Aircraft Radio Receiver was installed.

Occasionally we were allowed off the ship and just knowing the invasion was coming soon, made me appreciate every second I had.

> *May 1, 1944*—Yesterday was beautiful spring weather. I enjoyed just strolling through beautiful Ralph Park in Cardiff. The fellows were disgusted because all the pubs, shows, and cafes were closed. We did find a Greek cafe open and had rabbit and chips. When we came out, I noticed a sign on the next building which read "Cat and Dog Meat for Sale." It started my mind wondering.
>
> We passed a gypsy fortune teller, and one of the fellows decided to have his fortune told. It was a filthy dive. She wanted to bless my shipmate's money, but he wasn't so foolish as to give her the wallet. He handed her two and six and walked out.
>
> I went to the Red Cross for coffee and sandwiches and cabled my mother for Mother's Day. A little while later, I met my three buddies in town minus the girls they had picked up. We returned to the ship tired.

In early May, forty-three new men came aboard the USS *LST-388*. They had come from the States aboard the big Cunard liner, RMS *Queen Mary*. I had often admired this ship when she sailed into New York harbor.

Training was taking place in every part of the United Kingdom, from Northern Ireland, to Scotland, to Wales, to England. Our ship remained in Wales and continued with assigned training, drills, and firing practice. On May 5, 1944, an order came through for myself and one other radioman to attend training for the new radar system. We left the ship and wouldn't return for ten days.

RMS Queen Mary

The RMS *Queen Mary* was fast, having broken the speed record for a North Atlantic crossing. She traversed the 3,088 miles from Cherbourg, France, to Ambrose Lightship (outside New York harbor) in 4 days, 8 hours, and 37 minutes at an average speed of 29.61 knots. An LST averaged about 8 to 10 knots.

Drastically refitted for World War II, the *Queen Mary* boosted her 2,000-passenger capacity to 15,000 —a full division. Though Adolph Hitler offered $250,000 and the Iron Cross (Germany's highest award for bravery) for her sinking, she transported 765,429 troops unscathed. She was seldom escorted. [Life magazine, Vol. 63, No. 14, Oct. 6, 1967, *Out to Sea and Into History*)

The Queen Mary is 1018 feet long. At age thirty-one, the lovely liner was retired by her owners, the Cunard Line. New York, which welcomed her 1,000 times, bid the grand old lady a raucous farewell as thousands lined the shore. I lived in Staten Island on September 22, 1967, and took my family down to Von Briesen Park overlooking The Narrows. A large crowd had gathered to watch the Queen Mary go under the Verrazano-Narrows Bridge and out New York harbor for the last time. The Queen Mary is now docked in Long Beach, California, and is used as a floating hotel.

May 18, 1944—A few weeks ago, I was sent from Milford Haven, Wales, to Falmouth, England, to attend radar school. The trip by train was quite arduous as there were many changes made. I had to pass through Cardiff, Bristol, Plymouth, and Truro. Another radioman, Stocks, and I arrived in Plymouth about midnight, and all the beds at the Red Cross were taken. The only place left to go was a British Servicemen's Club. It proved to be rather dirty, but it was a bed.

When I awoke in the morning, there seemed to be a league of nations sleeping in the bunks nearby. There were British, New Zealanders, Dutchmen, etc. Stocks and I spent the morning in Plymouth and caught the one-thirty train to Falmouth.

We arrived in Falmouth at about four o'clock on Saturday afternoon, but the school did not start until Monday. They took us to a place called Beacon Hill, and there we bunked in a Quonset hut with other radio and radar men who were also to attend the school. The chow was in a huge mess hall and wasn't too good. We had the entire weekend to ourselves but no place to go.

We took a ride to Truro but found it just as overcrowded as Falmouth. I went to Truro just to see the large cathedral, which dominates the town. It is impressive, and seeing this beautiful church made my trip worthwhile.

Sunday, the only thing going was a Red Cross tea dance. I met a pretty redhead who was in the British WAAF [Women's Auxiliary Air Force]. After several dances, Stocks and I left with the girls. They took us to a little restaurant where we bought a fairly nice supper. After the meal, we walked through the park before they had to catch a bus for Redruth where they were stationed.

Sometimes I wonder if this invasion is ever going to come off. Let's have it and get it over with.

On Wednesday evening, Stocks managed to get some British rum. We both drank quite a bit of it before meeting the girls again. We took them to supper. After supper, there was nothing to do but walk along the seashore. My girl, Joan, proved to be a very nice person. We talked a lot about our plans for the future and so forth. The four of us then went to a dance at an old hotel called the Princess Pavilion. It was surrounded by beautiful gardens. The girls had to leave immediately after the dance to ride back to camp with the band.

While at the Red Cross on Sunday, Joe Louis, the heavyweight boxing champ [and sergeant in the US Army], sat at a table next to ours. He was a popular champion. Louis said that he believed we would win the war because "God is on our side."

On Monday, we were detached from radar school and sent back to our ship. The USS *LST-388* was moored about an hour's ride up the River Fal. Steep hills went up on each side of the river making it a good hiding place for LSTs. When we returned to the ship, we found that forty men had been added to the crew. It seemed like a new ship.

Everyone feels the invasion will start real soon. If they put any more American equipment and men on the British Isles, they might sink. Guess I should be worried about the dangers ahead of us, but I am not. I lived through Salerno, so I guess I can live through this.

In mid-May, as a precautionary measure, chemical defense supplies were brought on board our ship. These included 102 gas masks, 268 eye shields, as well as gas detectors. Army gas masks were issued to everyone on the ship. All inoculations were brought up to date. Everything was being checked, from the boiler to the barrage balloon equipment. As with past invasions, all service and health records for ship's personnel were sent ashore to the Operations Office for safe keeping. Army medical personal came aboard and would stay throughout the invasion as our ship had been designated as a casualty ship. This meant we would be one of the ships designated to carry the wounded back to England for treatment.

The invasion had been delayed, more than once, due to the forecasted weather, but also due to the lack of available LSTs. (Many accounts written after the war mention that the shortage of LSTs was problematic.) Now that our ship and others like her had proven their value in the invasions on Sicily and Salerno, the importance of LSTs was well noted. We had been tested over and over again, and had come through as reliable and necessary. We were proud of our ship, and our crew, and our service. And now, it was time to do it all again.

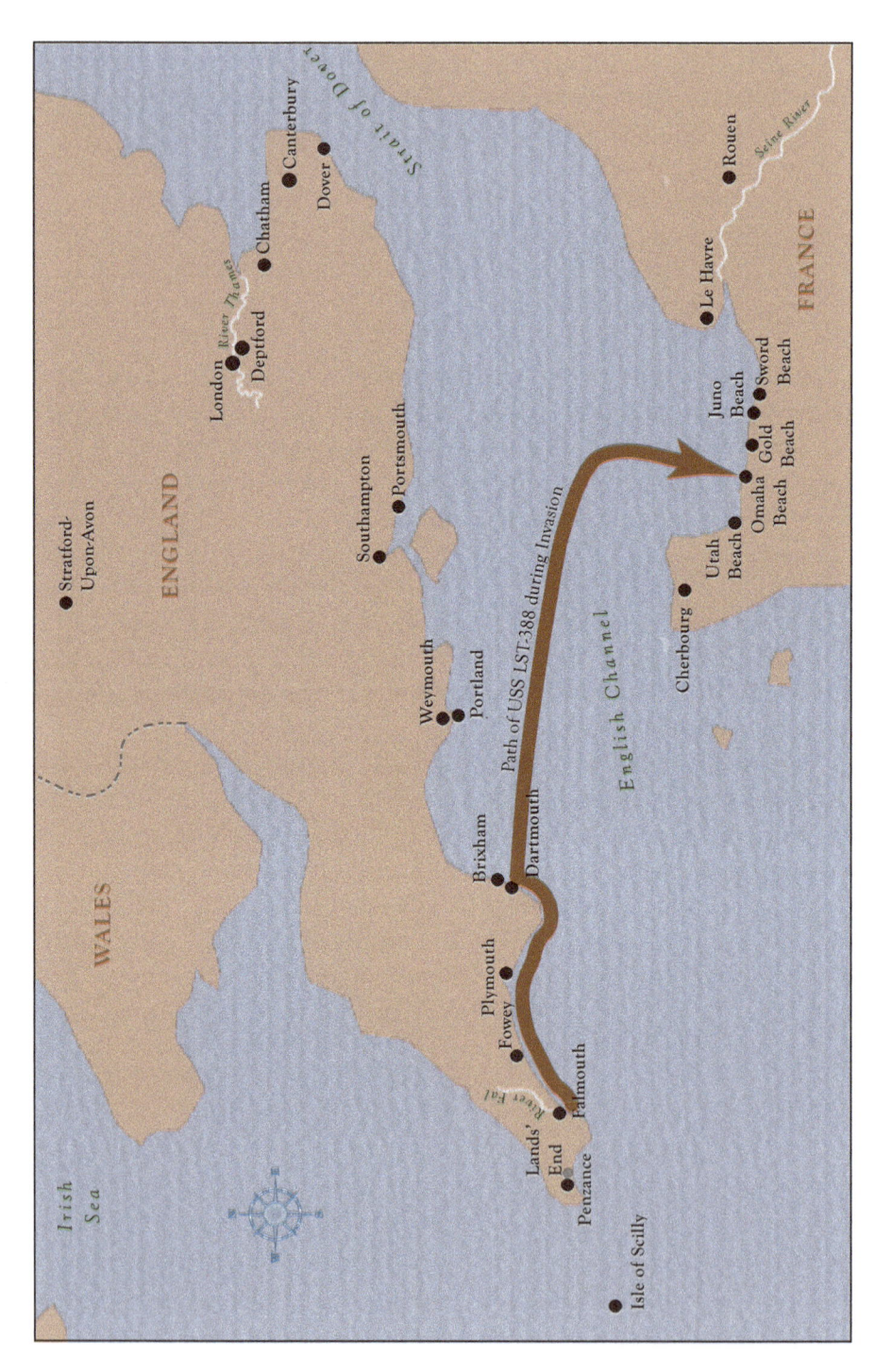

D-Day: The Invasion of France
Code Name: *Neptune/Overlord*

THE INVASION OF FRANCE was set to take place at Normandy, along five beaches: Utah, Omaha, Gold, Juno and Sword. The British and Canadians would land at Gold, Juno and Sword. The Americans would land at Utah and Omaha.

May 31, 1944—Plymouth, England. I was to have liberty today but, as the weather is bad, I gave it to Stocks, another radioman. We have been told the ship is sealed, and the first phase of the operation has started. No enlisted man can go ashore unless escorted by an officer.

This evening, we moved out to the outer bay and waited for the morning sail to Falmouth. Ships are crammed in Plymouth harbor like sardines in a can.

June 1, 1944—Today we sailed, arriving at Falmouth without incident.

June 2, 1944—We went up to a hard on the River Fal to load the 187th Field Artillery with their 155mm guns. In the evening, we pulled out and anchored near Falmouth itself. I had the 2000 to 2400 signal watch. It was a beautiful evening. Darkness came about ten o'clock, and the moon shone bright. On a hill a short distance away, cows grazed. The Cornwall countryside is beautiful in the moonlight. How peaceful it seems. Hundreds of barrage balloons are overhead. We rather expected an air attack, but none came.

June 3, 1944—In port, waiting for order to join convoy. This afternoon, the crew was issued impregnated clothing for use in the event of a gas attack.

June 4, 1944—We got underway at daybreak with a pontoon barge in tow. The weather started to act up, and the sea became very choppy. The convoy was ordered to return to Falmouth harbor. We were informed that the USS *LST-388* is not in the initial assault wave. The USS *LST-388* will beach at D plus one. It rained today.

Our ship was to be part of Force "B", following closely behind Force "O" (Omaha) and Force "U" (Utah), and bound for Omaha Beach. The plan was to provide an immediate, immense follow-up of troops and guns in order to overwhelm the Germans.[17] Force "B" contained four convoys. The USS *LST-388* would sail in one of those convoys, along with 33 other LSTs.

June 5, 1944—We set sail again for our destination in France. The convoy proceeded slowly up the coast. There were LSTs as far as one could see as well as ships from the American, English, French, Dutch [as well as other countries] navies, and liberty ships by the scores. As we passed Fowey, more LSTs joined our convoy. During the day, we saw hundreds of planes.

June 6, 1944—This is D-Day. In a way, I wish we were scheduled to hit the beach today. Can't say that I am scared, just a little anxious. We are anxious to hear how the initial assault wave is making out. They have us on four-on-four-off watches still. In our compartment, there are four empty bunks, so four soldiers have been assigned to them. We have 500 men on board. Besides the 187th, we have Headquarters Companies B and C and a medics unit. They are all swell fellows, and the soldiers are well versed in the detailed plans for the invasion. All of us are becoming quite friendly. The troops sure are in good spirits.

News came that the initial assault has been successful and proceeding according to plan. [What else would you expect them to say?] We saw much gunfire ahead.

In the evening, hundreds of ships, many big transports, could be seen heading back to England, empty.

June 7, 1944—We are close off the invasion coast. The number of ships around us is unbelievable! Battleships, cruisers, and destroyers are still throwing in salvo after salvo [simultaneous firing of artillery]. Every once in a while, a shore battery opens up. Several shells fell not too far from us. We are all wondering where the German Air Force is.

Our group anchored off Vierville-sur-Mer while awaiting our turn to hit the beach and unload. The warships scored several direct hits on German ammunition and storage dumps not far from us. Huge flames and clouds of smoke lifted into the sky. Through glasses, we can see that the shore is a beehive of activity.

During the night, we fired all our guns during an air raid, and they say seven planes were shot down. There were several E-boat attacks in the western part of our sector. All were driven off without loss to any ships in our area. All ships laid down smoke immediately.

Besides mines, the beaches are blocked with concrete piles, wire, pillboxes, foxholes, and cross-iron railings. All of these are clearly visible, especially at low tide.

June 8, 1944—We were ordered onto the beach at high tide. Everyone was wondering what Jerry [Germany] was doing with his planes. At about two-thirty, we eased ourselves to the beach. As the tide went out, we were left high and dry on Omaha Beach. The number of broached boats [boats heeled too far to one side, or capsized] of every description is unbelievable. Masses of equipment are strewn all along the shore for miles, equipment left behind during enemy action or destroyed by the choppy sea. It reminds me of the beach at Salerno.

The LCT-305 off to our right is a miserable wreck, broken in two. This is the same LCT we carried to England from Bizerte. I wonder what happened to her crew. I know them all quite well. To our port, is the wreckage of LCI-553 [landing craft, infantry] on which a friend of mine from radar school served. Some of the dead are still lying as they fell.

As the tide went out, more scenes were revealed. Landmines went off every few minutes. We lowered our ramp very close to a land mine [about two feet]. A tractor carrier towing a 155mm gun pulled out of the ramp about a hundred yards and hit another mine. The two men in it flew straight up in the air. Both of the men are badly hurt. They are still alive, though, for they carried them back on board.

Another mine went off on our starboard side, and pieces hit the conning tower, not two feet from where I was standing. Not far from the bow door, lay a dead American floating back and forth, face down, with the waves. Up a ways, a German soldier lay with his middle missing.

They began bringing the wounded aboard. We had already received several onboard the previous evening. The wounded are English, American, and German. The wardroom has been made into an operating room. Some of these men say that the Americans met two Nazi divisions on maneuvers. The landing operations were horrific in the Omaha [Beach] sector. The Germans slaughtered many with mortar and machine-gun fire as the Allied soldiers hit the beach. Every house had a sniper. Sometimes the snipers were French. French women dressed in Nazi uniforms and acting as snipers. Landmines were all over the place.

On *June 9, 1944*, the USS *LST-388* pulled off the beach at high tide and anchored about a mile out. There were several air raids during the night, but the raid about 12:30 A.M. seemed the heaviest. Several planes could be seen going down in flames. Some of those lost were ours. Several barrage balloons also went down in flames. We received warning by radio to be on alert for E-boats as well.

On our second trip to the beach, we carried Americans. Just before we arrived in the Utah Assault Area, in Normandy, an LST to our port hit a mine and began to sink. Soldiers started jumping over the sides. Ships sent small boats. Since she was settling slowly when we last saw her, I doubt that there were too many casualties.

I will never forget our second trip back to England. The USS *LST-388* was really a hospital ship. It carried several hundred wounded. They

D-DAY: THE INVASION OF FRANCE

Our troops proved Hitler wrong again. Albert Speer, in his book *Inside the Third Reich*, wrote, "Hitler clung to the end to his preconceived opinion that the troops of the Western countries were poor fighting material. Even the Allied successes in Africa and Italy could not shake his belief that these soldiers would run away from the first serious onslaught. He was convinced that democracy enfeebled a nation."

Later in his book, Speer states that on June 6, 1944, when the invasion of Europe began, Hitler thought it was a feigned attack in order to divert him from the true invasion site and try to lure him into committing his divisions too soon in the wrong place. He rejected his original, accurate view that the coast of Normandy would most likely be the focus of the invasion.

Source: Speer, Albert, *Inside the Third Reich: Memoirs*, translated from the German by Richard and Clara Winston, Bonanza Books, New York, 1982, p. 306.

---

were brought aboard from ducks [amphibious vehicles], LCVPs [landing craft, vehicle and personnel], and LCTs [landing craft, tank]. I helped carry the litters [stretchers] and lay them on the tank deck. Many of the wounded hadn't eaten in days and were hardly given more than first-aid. Many had very serious injuries. It was hard to stay on the tank deck very long and hear the wounded moan and cry in pain.

Our three doctors and twenty corpsmen were very busy all the way back to England. Their operating table was a mess table or a litter stretched across two horses. Many amputations took place while the ship rolled. Most of the wounded tried to help themselves, but others were too bad off to even move a blanket. Many were parachute troops who claimed not to have taken prisoners since the Germans had strung up some of their men.

Tom Bernard, United States Navy Reserve and navy correspondent wrote an article in the *Yank, The Army Weekly* news magazine, called "Hospital in a Hold." A picture of USS *LST-388* was featured as she sat high and dry on the beach. In the article, Bernard said of LSTs, "Floating boxcars—some skippers called them contemptuously—but that was in the days when it was thought that a Landing Ship Tank merely landed tanks. Then someone realized that there would be a lot of empty space that could be used to carry wounded back across the Channel and treat them en route. The medical equipment may be jury-rigged, but the fact remains that LSTs have proved a lifesaving boon to many an injured fighter being evacuated from France this summer."

Source: *Yank, The Army Weekly*, Vol. 3, No. 8, 1944.

As soon as the beachheads had been secured by the Allies, the build-up of troops and supplies increased immediately. We continued our shuttle of troops, vehicles, guns, ammunition and supplies across the Channel, returning back to England with the wounded. Since no harbor had yet been established, we continued the method of "drying out" on the beaches, or beaching and waiting for the tide to go out so we could unload our cargo directly on the beaches themselves—no need for pontoon causeways, rhino barges, or unloading onto smaller landing craft for delivery to the beach. Then, when the tide came in, we eased off the beach and either anchored out at sea, or joined a convoy sailing back to England for yet another load of reinforcements or supplies.

Unloading by the "drying-out" method took about 10–12 hours, as timing coincided with the tides. To show what this timing looked like, on June 12, 1944, we beached in the Utah Assault Area at 0410, and unloaded between 0730 and 0825. At 1340, high tide, we pulled off the beach and anchored a mile out.

The USS *LST-388* sits on the beach at Normandy. In the forefront is sister ship, USS *LST-325*, which was found and sailed back from Greece in 2000. It now sits on the Ohio River in Evansville, Indiana as a ship memorial. This photo appeared in several articles including *Neptune Flops on the Job: The U.S. Navy Gets a Stand-Up From Davy Jones*, and the article *Hospital in a Hold*.

Minesweepers continued their non-stop sweep off the beaches but they couldn't get to them all. USS *LST-499* found one for them and was badly damaged, as did other types of ships.

The German E-boat threat remained in the Channel, which we crossed night and day in follow up trips for the build-up on the beaches. The Germans still controlled the port of Cherbourg where the E-boats were based and they would be ordered out at night to hunt for Allied ships.

Air raids still occurred, and usually when least expected. Whenever an LST was high and dry on a beach, it undoubtedly made a tempting target. On the 16th of June, five US Navy LSTs beached at British Sword Beach. Shortly afterwards, German shellfire rained down on them. They continued unloading, and all they could do then was wait for the rising tide to take them back out to sea. Remarkably, only five shots hit the ships, and there were very few casualties.

And one cannot forget the weather, which was always a formidable foe in the English Channel. One storm in particular, between June 19th and 22nd, brought almost all activity to a halt. It was said to be the worst June storm in over 40 years.

We were not assigned to one particular beach, but instead shuttled troops and supplies to all the beaches, including the British Beaches. The logistics of these convoys must have been some kind of nightmare to plan. Between D-Day and the end of June, we had already made six trips across the Channel.

> *June 28, 1944*—We have made two trips to the British beach [Juno] carrying both British and Canadian troops. These fellows are very friendly. They liked our ship mainly because the American chow is better than what they usually receive. Both times we unloaded at night. There were frequent air raids during the night, and we saw quite a few planes shot down.
>
> We are now back on Utah Beach with our fourth load of Americans. Just behind us are two sunken LSTs, one with part of its bow sticking out of the water and the other laying on its side. A liberty ship is nearby with only its bow sticking high in the air.

When we returned to England from our sixth trip, we carried 592 prisoners. They were marched into the tank deck and were guarded by a few soldiers. The prisoners had been marched nine miles to reach the ship. As I was on radio watch, I did not get down to see them until we were underway. When I opened the hatch leading to the tank deck, there was a terrible smell of humanity. The Germans were crammed in the tank deck like sardines. We were told not to trade with them, but some sailors got $35 in francs for a few packages of cigarettes. They cashed the francs for pounds in England. Many got German marks for souvenirs.

I walked the length of the tank deck and looked over the prisoners. They were all ages. None seemed particularly interested in me. Guess I looked too much like them. They didn't look like men who could commit all the crimes the Germans are accused of. But then again, you can't tell a book by its cover. The British took over the

D-DAY: THE INVASION OF FRANCE

German prisoners disembarking from the USS *LST-388* at Southampton, England.

prisoners at Southampton. We had trouble with the bow anchor, so we stayed in port a few days. Liberty in the bomb-shattered town of Southampton wasn't much to write about.

Once repairs to the bow anchor were complete, we loaded British troops and vehicles and once again sailed for Normandy, this time to Gold Beach. We quickly returned to Southampton to load the US Army Quartermaster Corp and Quartermaster Truck Co. They were needed at Omaha Beach. While loading their vehicles, on July 8, 1944, we learned that USS *LST-384* and USS *LST-312* were hit by a buzz bomb in Deptford, near London. The USS *LST-384* had been our training ship back on the Chesapeake Bay.

The first of these flying bombs [V-1, or buzz bomb] had reached London back on June 12th and continued to wreak havoc on the city, and our ships. The V-1 is really a small pilotless airplane, which flies at high speed on a predetermined course and terminates its flight by settings in its mechanism. It contains a large number of explosives that detonate with a terrific blast upon contact with an object or the ground. The British called them *buzz bombs* because of their distinct buzzing sound.

USS *LST-388* on the beach at Normandy, with barrage balloon.

Once fully loaded again, we proceeded to the Omaha Assault Area, arriving on July 9th. By now we were accustomed to our common routine of unloading, retracting from the beach as the tide came in, then anchoring out from the beach to await orders to join a convoy back to England. On this particular return trip to England, however, the ship's steering went out and we had to switch to hand steering. It wasn't long however until our top-notch engineering group had made repairs, and we were back to mechanized steering. That group really had their work cut out for them, keeping the ship running, especially in the gale force winds and rough seas we encountered that day, and on many days to follow.

Back in port, we loaded waiting troops and equipment, and this time headed to the Utah Assault Area, landing on the beach known as Sugar Red Beach. We didn't get everything unloaded by the time the tide came in so we anchored off the beach and waited for the next

USS *LST-388* on the beach at Normandy.

tide. After completing the unloading, members of the 101st Airborne Division came aboard for transport back to England.

July 14, 1944, on the beach in Normandy-Omaha—On our last return trip to England, we carried airborne troops. They sure were happy to get aboard. When we got to the hard in England, there was a band to meet them. They proudly displayed a captured Nazi flag, which they hung on the side of the ship when we came in. You would think they were getting back to the States they were so happy. These troops really went through a lot. They claimed that over a third of this force was lost. We had 360 of them on board.

When we returned to England this time, we were ordered to sail to Portland. We anchored in Weymouth Bay, just outside Portland, and remained in port awaiting a decision as to whether our ship was

View of invasion fleet at Normandy.

Build-up on the Normandy beaches begins. LSTs landing vehicles and cargo on a Normandy beach, June 8, 1944.

View from the USS LST-388, at Utah Beach, Normandy.

USS *LST-388* weather deck loaded with Army troops, vehicles and supplies on the way to Normandy.

LST 388

USS *LST-388* with bow doors open and ramp down, on a Normandy beach.

Reinforcements of men and equipment moving inland at Normandy. LSTs are anchored just off the beach.

Normandy—taking wounded aboard for trip back to England.

A mine too close to the USS *LST-388* bow door while on the beach at Normandy.

The mine being removed on the beach at Normandy.

considered operational or not. The condition of the ship's screws and shafts had come into question. We had worked her hard over the last month and a half, and she held up when we needed her to, but now she needed some attention.

Chatham

In mid-July, we passed through the Strait of Dover on our way from Portland to Chatham [near London] on the River Thames. We were to undergo ship repairs at the Royal Shipyard. Thirteen buzz bombs passed over the ship, several of them very low. Our ship did not fire at them in the dark but the shore batteries opened up with everything they had. British night-fighting aircraft even chased some of them.

As it turned out, we would spend the rest of the month of July in Chatham, and most of that time the ship was in dry-dock. We did have some of the best liberty since arriving in England while there however.

Chatham was a good-sized town with plenty of liquor, women, and hardly any Americans. It was an hour's train ride from London and although flying bombs were continuously going over the place, it seemed undamaged. On my first liberty here, I drank quite a bit and consequently had quite a hangover the next day.

On my second liberty, I went to London to see my friend Muriel Mountford. On the way, several flying bombs passed over. We were able to see the damage many of them did when they hit. About a block was cleared out by one of these bombs.

I found Muriel to be the same sweet girl I had known last January. When I arrived at her house, she had her uniform on and was just about to leave for her Red Cross station. Her post was in an underground [subway] station where hundreds of civilians went to sleep to get away from the menace of the buzz bombs. She volunteered to do this several times a week. As I walked to the station with her, we passed quite a few bombed-out buildings.

Muriel got an early excusal, and we went back to her house for tea. As we were drinking our tea and talking with her parents, an alert sounded. I could see her mother was scared, especially when we heard the loud noise of the bomb.

Although I explained that there was only a slight chance of my getting liberty again in time for Sunday dinner, Ms. Mountford insisted I try to make it. I tried to say no because of the strict rationing and the trouble it would cause her, but she insisted. They would wait as long as possible for me.

I got the last underground to Piccadilly from which I went to Waterloo station, then to London Bridge station to wait for the 3:15 train back to Chatham. While waiting at the London Bridge Station, a number of flying bombs came over. You could hear them loud overhead. Everyone got up from their seats and went to a shelter or looked for a safe place to hide from the glass in case the noise [similar to an outboard motor] were to stop. When the flame in the rear goes out, the bomb comes down. We saw the light go out and heard the noise stop on several occasions, and a few seconds later, there was a huge explosion and a tremendous flash of light not too far away. This bomb is really a terrible weapon.

Sunday, I had to disappoint the Mountfords for we were not allowed one-o'clock liberty because seven fellows did not get back from the last one. As soon as I did get liberty, I raced to the Mountfords' home. We had supper and Mrs. Mountford certainly treated me royally. She had a number of delicacies saved up. It made me feel strange that these people went so far out of their way to please me. I know they must have made many sacrifices to do so. After a while, Muriel and I walked through beautiful Finsbury Park not far from her home. We sat on a bench near the lake and talked while watching the ducks and ducklings. I think we both enjoyed our talk more than anything more exciting we could have done that night.

Before I took the last train back, I told her that I would probably not see her again unless she came to the States. I also told her that if I were to get a long enough leave, I would probably get married. She wished me all the luck in the world but said it wouldn't be right for her to correspond with me if I got married. I certainly hoped she would change her mind. My thoughts at the time were, is it wrong to have a girl merely as a friend even if I get married? Should marriage call a halt to friendships such as this? Muriel let me kiss her goodbye and I told her I would never forget her, and I haven't.

I did get two more liberties while at Chatham but did not go back to London. On one of those liberties, a buddy and I decided to stay in Chatham and take in a vaudeville show. Since we were a bit early, we decided to go upstairs to a bar and partake of a few. After about the second drink, a very lovely girl appeared and I got in a friendly conversation with her. I bought her a drink. She was pretty and built like you know what.

A little guy came up, said he was her manager and that she was in the show. The girl made us promise to meet her afterward. We agreed and went in to see the performance. The event was a real burlesque. Slouchy dressed comedians told corny English jokes; others danced and sang.

Then they announced that the star act of the evening was to be four scenes depicting the four seasons. As the orchestra played, a girl built for comfort and twice as pretty appeared in the nude. She was absolutely captivating. Then I looked again, and who do you think it was? Yes, it was my friend I had met at the bar and planned to see later.

My blood just about boiled in anticipation. Oh, if I could only round up the courage to meet this beauty. I bet it would be an interesting evening. Coward that I am, I left by the side door at the last minute. I saw her for a long time afterward—in my dreams.

On the last liberty while at Chatham, a buddy and I went to Canterbury for a quick but interesting sightseeing tour. A cab driver who knew the histories of all the sights, including the famous Norman Castle, took us around. We drove through the old gates in the wall surrounding the city. He pointed out places where the *Canterbury Tales*, written by Geoffrey Chaucer, supposedly took place. We also visited the Abby of St. Benedict where the old caretaker took us around. To top it off, we visited the badly damaged Canterbury Cathedral. The simple graves where Norman Kings were supposedly buried seemed odd to me.

Channel Crossings
Trains to Cherbourg

WITH OUR REPAIRS at the Royal Shipyard in Chatham complete, we set sail for Southampton, England. Upon arrival, we began making preparations to haul trains to Cherbourg, France by having tracks welded to our tank deck and ramp.

Motor convoys along the roads in France could no longer keep up with the supply needs of the troops, and rail was to be the answer. However, much of the railroad equipment in Europe had been destroyed by pre-invasion bombings.

Fortunately, prior to the invasion of Normandy, the US had the foresight to ship over 1,000 locomotives and approximately 20,000 railroad cars to the UK in anticipation of just such needs. The question then was how to get the rail cars to France without adequate deep-water ports, and port unloading equipment such as cranes.

It was the railway engineers who came up with the solution. They devised a plan to land the trains on the beaches in France by first laying railway tracks in the bottom of the LST's tank deck. Next, in Cherbourg, they laid railway tracks down to the beach, to the hards on the water's edge. When the LST beached, these ground tracks were connected to the tracks in the LST. The railway cars would simply roll out of the ships.[18]

The need for these trains was indeed great, as supplies had to get to the troops fighting in the interior, far away from the shores where

Above and below: Transporting trains from Southampton, England to Cherbourg France.

Above and below: Transporting trains from Southampton, England to Cherbourg France.

we could land. Cherbourg, France had been heavily defended and finally wrestled from the Germans on June 25, 1944, but the port had been badly damaged. Mines were everywhere, requiring several minesweepers and even deep-sea divers to dive down and disarm the mines on the bottom. The hazards were numerous. By the time we arrived with our first load of rail cars, only part of the port had been cleared enough for us to enter.

> *August 5, 1944*—We sailed from Southampton yesterday and arrived in Cherbourg, France today. The port city is much smaller than I imagined, and the Germans have about demolished the waterfront. It will be a long time before the Allies have this port operating at capacity again. Minesweepers are now sweeping the harbor. There are but a few docks that are operable. Supply ships are anchored in the harbor and unloading onto lighters [flat bottom barges].
>
> A large tug hit a mine in the inner harbor where we were and sank in a few minutes. She was only two ship lengths from our port side and about sixty feet from the hard where we unloaded.
>
> The Allies still have not taken a major port intact, which is essential to bringing in supplies. Most supplies are still being landed on the beaches.

The supplying of troops without adequate deep-water ports would continue to haunt the Allies. Fortunately, the back- up plan was always the use of LSTs drying out on a beach or pulling up to a concrete hard.

In just over three months, June 6th to September 15th, (1944), the Allied Armies had reached the German border, from the beaches of Normandy in France. From all I have read since the war, the Allied forces advanced so rapidly that they soon outran their supplies, which caused a slowdown in their advance. We did our part to get reinforcements, and the vehicles and supplies to the beaches and ports, but from there, it proved challenging to get them to the interior where the troops were. Fortunately, the train system was of great help.

During the months of August, September, October, and most of November, we volleyed between Southampton in England and Cherbourg in France, transporting the railway cars for the US Army Transportation Corp. On each trip, we carried anywhere from 13 to 20 railroad cars, from flat cars, to box cars, to 40-ton "gondolas." It became so routine that I didn't even bother to keep detailed notes in my journal.

Often, while underway, we would have to dodge minesweepers, merchant convoys, and an occasional out-of-control ship. The weather became an unpredictable factor as rough seas, gale force winds, rain and thick fog became even more common.

Aboard ship, attempts were made to keep us from becoming too complacent. Surprise formal and informal inspections took place, with a few of them requiring full scale fire drills, collision drills, and abandon ship drills.

Many times, while in port for loading, crew would be temporarily assigned to night Shore Patrol Duty, usually for about six or so hours at a time. The goal of the Shore Patrol was to maintain order wherever sailors and soldiers were on liberty, and keep them from getting too rowdy. I was assigned to a few of these, but fortunately not too many. Very few liberties were granted and I rarely got off the ship during these months. When I did, I, as always, did my best to take advantage of every second.

At the end of August, I was granted just such a leave for three days. I decided to return to London where I met a very nice Scotch lass named May who seemed to drink a lot of scotch. She was in the British Army ATS [Auxiliary Territorial Service, women's branch of the British Army], assigned to a gun battery in Scotland.

The next day, May claimed the reason she drank so much the night I met her was that she was upset after having broken up with her Jewish boyfriend so that he would not lose his inheritance. He was sent overseas with the British Intelligence the morning I met her. I accepted the story for what it was worth. We went to a Chinese restaurant and then to the dance at Covent Gardens. When we left the dance, it was past the curfew time at her billet, so I had a cab driver find her a hotel room. I couldn't summon the courage to go upstairs with her. I am sure it would have been rewarding.

LST 388

The next morning, I made my way to the Regent Park Zoo and Madame Tussauds Wax Works. Both places were enjoyable. At the Wax Works, the figures were so lifelike that at times I had to study them to make sure they were not real.

I took what I thought was an early train back to Southampton but missed the ship by two hours. Several of us waited around Southampton in very bad weather for five days before the ship came back. Most of the time we were at the local Red Cross.

A little later on I would receive another short, authorized leave, but it would turn into more of a nightmare than a liberty.

After liberty had been granted about six in the evening, three of us took an hour and a half ride in an open boat in a choppy sea to the landing. We were soaked from spray and drenched when a pouring rain came on us for twenty minutes. Chet, Wit, and I felt disgusted and began to drink anything that came along. We went pub crawling. Chet, the senior member of the group, was an old hand at this. He found pubs in the craziest places. Half the time, we walked through what seemed like ghost towns. Building after building was half-bombed-out; windows rattled, and the rain beat down. There wasn't a soul around. The bombings were all a year or more old.

Before we got feeling too high, we reserved bunks at the Red Cross. It was really foolish to drink so much, but we just didn't give a darn. Chet bought a [quart] bottle of rum for six pounds [approximately $24], which we put down our bellies in short order.

While walking along a deserted part of town, Chet just passed out, like a sack of beans. We draped him on a fence, but still we couldn't get him navigating. Finally, we stopped a jeep and I picked Chet up and set him head first into it. We rode through the center of town with Chet's feet sticking up in the air.

At the Red Cross, we poured Chet into his bunk and left him. Our bunks were on the next level. In the morning, we found out the MPs [military police] had taken Chet away because he caused a disturbance. The MPs had handed Chet over to the SPs [shore patrol] and they locked him up for the night in a telephone booth. When the phone kept ringing, Chet thought it was general quarters and started yelling for his helmet.

A fellow at the Red Cross the next morning gave Chet coffee and tried to clean him up a bit before he had to return to the ship.

But, by ship time, Chet and Wit had managed to buy another bottle and were pretty well lit up. I had had enough. Whenever Chet gets drunk, he starts reciting Shakespeare and Rudyard Kipling, such as [from "On the Road to Mandalay"]:

Ship me somewhere east of Suez, where the best is like the worst
Where there aren't no Ten Commandments an' a man can raise a thirst.

I was sure glad to catch the ship.

Chet was the oldest enlisted man on board. When sober, he was a very competent quartermaster. His hobby was researching the lost continent of Atlantis.

Back aboard ship, routine continued, yet not without occasional surprises. On one particular day, we were anchored in the harbor in England. In the early morning, the dense night fog had not yet fully dissipated. I was by myself on the conning tower on signal watch with not another person topside. All of a sudden, a huge ship appeared, bearing down on us dead ahead. It turned out to be an empty large oil tanker, but it scared me as it kept coming as if it didn't see us.

I jumped down to the wheelhouse and slammed down the alarm handle. When the alarm sounded, the crew came running, and the bulkhead door was sealed. At first, everyone thought it was an air raid, but when the officers got to the bridge, they saw this huge ship gliding past us only a few feet off our starboard side. He just missed us, and then disappeared into the fog. I didn't even see its name. The captain said I did the right thing in sounding the alarm. We had witnessed several ship collisions over the course of the war and knew not to take any chances.

Towards the end of November, after twenty-nine round trips between Southampton, England and Cherbourg, France transporting rail cars, we sailed for Weymouth, near Portland, England. We weren't finished yet, though. More reinforcements, tanks, and vehicles needed to get to France. We were old hands at this by now, yet you could never discount the possibility of something going wrong. Crossing the channel was always treated as a hazardous journey, regardless of what stage in the war we were.

On one of those Cross-Channel trips, a merchant ship erratically passed our convoy, then exploded. The ship started to list to starboard, and we prepared to lower our small boat to send out a rescue party. We were soon signaled, however, to steer clear of the damaged ship while a small coastal freighter came out to pick up survivors. Then a second explosion occurred and the ship sank rapidly.

As the winter approached, the weather deteriorated even more in the English Channel. Thick fog, strong seas, and high winds threatened moorings, maneuvering, loading, and unloading. Congested harbors didn't help. On one particular foggy morning, as we proceeded in to Portland Harbor to load army troops, we encountered the British ship, HMS *King Emperor*, exiting. Seeing that collision was imminent, our ship made all efforts to avoid, but to no avail. That ship's bow hit our ship between frames 12 and 13 on the starboard bow. Although the shell plating was pierced and deeply dented, we were lucky. Shortly afterwards, we moved away from the harbor entrance to assess the damage and let the British ship exit.

Christmas 1944

During Christmas 1944, we were still engaged in ferrying troops and equipment across the English Channel, and the job was so routine I didn't bother taking notes. The element of danger from submarines or air raids seemed hardly to exist.

Little did we realize that real danger was all around us. The Germans had launched their last desperate offensive, called the Battle of the Bulge, and the German Navy coordinated its activities to coincide with the attack.

Not until I read the *Veterans of Foreign Wars* (VFW) magazine of December 1988 did I realize how hazardous it really was to operate in the English Channel at that time.

A week after the Germans began the Battle of the Bulge in Belgium, France, and Luxemburg, more than 750 Americans of the 66th

Infantry Division were lost when their troopship, SS *Leopoldville*, was torpedoed, off Cherbourg, France. The U-486, a new snorkel-type U-boat, found its mark on Christmas Eve. The submarine had been ordered to a position near Cherbourg, France, to prevent Allied ships from carrying reinforcements to our hard-pressed troops. On December 26th, the same submarine sank two British escort vessels in the same area.[19]

It just so happened that my ship was underway for Cherbourg on that Christmas day, arriving there on the 26th. We had somehow just missed the danger.

Seine River Ports

The lack of available deep-water ports continued to plague the Allies. Fortunately, two shallow ports were captured on the Seine River, at Le Havre and Rouen, allowing us to get reinforcements, tanks, and vehicles further inland for the troops.

Le Havre sat at the opening to the Seine River. Rouen lay some seventy-five miles inland from Le Havre.

We took troops to Le Havre, France, and landed on the beach just inside the harbor. The port, as seen from our landing site, was totally destroyed, and like Cherbourg, it would be months before they could use this port to any great extent. No liberty was granted. What was the matter with the captain? Didn't he trust us with those French damsels?

That same winter, we also took troops up the Seine River to Rouen, France. I believe these were the reinforcements needed in the Battle of the Bulge. Much of the land on each side is let out in pasture and quite pretty. Along the way, we saw many bombed-out towns and shipyards and passed two sunken LSTs. On arriving at Rouen, we found the city heavily damaged by bombs. A huge cathedral seemed to dominate the area near the landing hard. Again, we were not permitted liberty.

As it turns out, the French in these towns where none too happy with the damage inflicted on their towns and held some animosity towards the Allies. Having any kind of liberty here would have been

Early 1945 LSTs unloading guns.

questionable. Besides, our trips up the Seine River to Rouen were well planned, and our stay short. Not long after unloading each time, we were sailing back downstream towards Le Havre, no doubt keeping the river clear for the next LSTs.

Another New Year arrived and we found ourselves once again moored in Portland, England, preparing to get underway to La Havre, France, with troops and vehicles already loaded. We continued transporting troops and vehicles, back and forth across the channel, all month long. February was more of the same, with heavy fog limiting visibility at times and requiring the installation of new radar equipment on our ship.

We did have occasional accidents aboard ship. One day a sailor was repairing one of the life boats and fell over the side. He was quickly retrieved by our small boat. On another day, we were tied up to a pier in England and the deck crew had to shorten up the lines when the tide came in. We had continuous gun watches in this port and for some reason, I was made a member of the bow 40mm gun crew. I guess the regular gun crew was on liberty or on a working party. As the deck gang shortened the cable of the forward spring line, it broke and snapped across the deck like a whip hitting the shield surrounding our gun mount. It scared me, but I felt horrified when I saw that that cable had caught one of the deck crew in the legs. He laid there screaming with two badly mangled legs. To this day, I often wonder if he was ever able to walk again.

I heard from home that a friend of mine, Walter Kyle, from St. John's Lutheran Church on Staten Island, had been wounded in France, and the army hospital he was in wasn't too far from where the ship was moored. I found the hospital after taking a train and hitchhiking, and it seemed well kept and organized. Italian prisoners worked as groundskeepers. Even though there were many recently constructed wooden barracks, it didn't take me long to find Walter. A shell fragment had hit him in the leg, I believe. I was happy to see he didn't have a more serious wound. He was glad to see someone from home, and I wrote Walter's family after the visit.

In what was to be my last real sightseeing liberty in England, a forty-eight-hour one, I decided to visit Penzance. Penzance is the last town in southern England and a short distance from Land's End, the most southern tip of England. I took a bus and enjoyed the countryside.

In my travels, I met a lovely English girl and her brother, visiting from their home on the Isles of Scilly. She helped me get a room at a quaint little inn even though she seemed a little leery of American sailors. I wonder why?

Penzance is still an old storybook town, and St. Michael's Mount, an island off the coast, presents a scene painters dream about.

After breakfast at the little inn, we rented some bicycles and had a pleasant ride to Land's End. It is a strange place, just the fields, the sharp cliffs, and the sea. A perfect place for our picnic. On the way back, we stopped at an old English pub, and the old lady who ran it had a parrot that talked.

In the afternoon, I saw my lady friend and her brother off on a little steamer that was to take them back home to the Isles of Scilly. I hated

Bridge Gang aboard the USS *LST-388*.

to see them go. I walked down the stone quay and found a shop where I bought two small watercolors and some postcards as mementos.

During the late spring of 1945, my notes became even more sparse and it seemed as if there was nothing new to report. The old USS *LST-388* just kept sailing along. Even liberties became monotonous. We all had had enough and yearned to get home to the States.

The LST class of ships had gone above and beyond what was hoped for and we were proud of our ship. After three invasions, and so many crossings between North Africa and Sicily, North Africa and the Italian mainland, and England and France, it's a wonder she still sailed. Our crew had been dedicated to keeping her running. She was, after all, our home.

Eventually we reported to Falmouth for ship repairs and general maintenance. While there, the ship received an overhaul of the main and auxiliary engines, and replacement of damaged plates on port and starboard bow. The rails on the tank deck were removed, and skids were added to the main deck for transport of an LCT. It was obvious the ship was being prepared for an ocean voyage. All English currency and banknotes were collected for conversion to American currency.

In early May we sailed to Belfast, Northern Ireland. It was here we found ourselves on May 8, 1945, better known as V-E Day, or Victory in Europe Day. The Germans had finally surrendered.

"Various exhibitions of fireworks and incandescent light throughout harbor and shore line. It was inferred that these were manifestations of the delight which the allied victory in Europe inspired. Naval propriety notwithstanding, all hands assembled to similarly express their exhilaration. Signals indicative of every genus of distress known to the nautical and naval world were dispatched with the aid of Verys pistols, Mersigs lights, the ship's whistle, and the signal lights. A ___ recurrent signal, V E, could not be decoded but in the interests of naval entries, it was repeated by this ship upon each rendition thereof by the surrounding ships. Onward America! Advance Brittania! Viva la France! Forward Russia!"

D. B. McKnight
Deck Log, USS LST-388
May 8, 1945 2200 hours

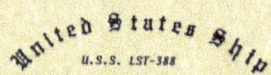

USS *LST-388* Ship Certificate of Service.

The Long Voyage Home

I N THE VERY EARLY MORNING HOURS of May 12, 1945, our convoy formed, and we began our long, slow trip back home. We departed Belfast, Northern Ireland, destined for Norfolk, Virginia.

The crew celebrated onboard by mixing drinks made up of orange juice and alcohol; the origin of the drinks' contents no one seemed to know. Speculation as to the future of the USS *LST-388* became the favorite topic of conversation.

The trip back to the States took about three weeks, traveling the northern route. Everyone was in a great mood with the prospects of getting home. The new miracle of radar enabled us to continue at the top speed of ten knots even though fog surrounded us the majority of the trip. The radar screen showed the position of every ship in the convoy. Our convoy, consisting of twelve LSTs, was the first to cross the Atlantic since the war in Europe had ended. From time to time, radio silence was broken. The trip home could be called routine—no breakdowns took place, no reports or sightings of icebergs near us.

We arrived in Norfolk, Virginia, on a clear day. I was sent ashore for the ship's mail, and as soon as I made it to shore, I phoned home and was thrilled to hear mom and dad's voices.

I don't know about the rest of the crew, but I thought we would receive a welcome of some kind after being overseas for more than two years. We proudly flew our homecoming pennant but received no welcome at all. Liberty was not granted in Norfolk.

The convoy was split up, sending six ships to New Orleans and six to New York for refitting to be of service in the Pacific Theater of War. Of course, I was hoping we would be sent to New York as it was my home. But, you guessed it! They sent the USS *LST-388* to New Orleans, Louisiana.

New Orleans, Louisiana

The trip to New Orleans began June 2, 1945, and took several days. It was miserably hot and humid as we traveled around the Florida peninsula and across the Gulf of Mexico. Sweat, sweat, sweat. We arrived at the mouth of the Mississippi River and obtained a pilot to navigate its twists and turns and currents. It seemed like a long trip up the Mississippi to New Orleans. The Mississippi was much bigger than the River Seine in France, and the muddy water of the river amazed me. Half the plains must be washing out to sea. The bayous on each side seemed barely inhabited.

On arrival, we tied up at the navy docks in Algiers, across the river from New Orleans. We sweated there a few days until we completely unloaded the ship. When everything, including our personal belongings, was ashore, we were granted a thirty-day leave—the first month's leave I ever had.

I took a train to New York as soon as I could get one, but no direct route existed. I changed trains in Washington, DC, and then boarded a Pennsylvania Railroad train that brought me to Pennsylvania Station in Manhattan.

Marriage

While on this thirty-day leave, Marge Ferenczi and I married. We had been more or less going steady before I went into the service, and we wrote to each other all the time I was overseas. The marriage took place in St. John's Lutheran Church, followed by a reception at the Clove Lakes Inn in the park. After the reception, we spent the

Above: Portrait of Robert von der Osten,

Left: Amphibious Force Patch and RM 1/C patch.

night at a Manhattan hotel. The next morning, we took a train to Lake George, New York, and had a most enjoyable week.

I hesitate to talk more about my marriage because it ended fifteen years later in a heartbreaking divorce.

Brodie Rig

In July 1945, I traveled back to New Orleans and was amazed to find the USS *LST-388* now had two masts with a long boom attached to the top of each. Our LST now served as a peculiar-looking aircraft carrier. Light planes were to land on a wire strung between the two booms and then be lowered to the deck.

To take off, Piper Clubs were suspended from this same wire and held back by a nylon rope. When the pilot revved up his motor, the plane dashed to the end of the wire, dropped off the wire, and was airborne. They called it a Brodie Rig.

We stayed in New Orleans for several weeks completing repairs, and I had liberty every night. Quite a few fellows had married while on leave and brought their wives to New Orleans. I felt the city was a good place to visit but not to live. It rained every day. I enjoyed the places like the Old Absinthe House and French Quarter. We ate at Antoine's, a famous French restaurant. The amusement park called Pontchartrain Beach, on the shore of Lake Pontchartrain, was a real fun place.

When ship repairs were completed, we went into the Gulf of Mexico to practice our new mission. We also did some anti-aircraft shooting at a sleeve towed by a plane. I had to talk to the pilot and could hardly hear him. I don't think he trusted us for he stayed quite far off.

The take-off and landing of two planes on board was quite successful in calm weather, but a PT boat rode alongside to act as a crash boat in the event one of the planes missed the hook.

While practicing maneuvers in the Gulf, we often went into the port of Galveston, Texas, for the night. The city seemed to be almost at water level. There were plenty of girls to be had, and many of the men hooked up with a bar girl or two. I guess some things never change.

The Atomic Bomb

On August 6, 1945, the atomic bomb was dropped on Hiroshima, Japan. It had the power of 20,000 tons of dynamite, and everything for miles around was burned to a crisp. We all talked about this terrible event and wondered what the Japanese would do. I don't think the average sailor realized what a terrible device had been invented. Meanwhile, ship's routine went on as usual. The United States warned Japan that she must surrender. We really bent our ear to every news broadcast we could.

The Japanese stalled in answering the call to surrender, and on August 9, 1945, a second atomic bomb was dropped, this time on Nagasaki, Japan. Russia declared war on Japan and crossed the Manchurian border.

On August 15, 1945, Japan decided to surrender. Emperor Hirohito broadcast the news to the Japanese people, and President Harry S. Truman declared the war over. We celebrated V—J (Victory—Japan) Day aboard ship, again, as best we could, and I would write one more entry in my journal.

> **August 15, 1945**—It is hard to believe the war is over. I have been on this ship so long that to call somewhere else home is going to be strange for a while.

The Point System

When we got back to New Orleans, on or about August 29, 1945, we received orders to sail for the [Panama] Canal Zone and passage to the Pacific. The navy announced the mustering-out point system. Married men received ten extra points. A survey of the crew revealed that I was the only one aboard who had enough points for discharge. I was twenty-five years old.

The yeoman typed a letter to the base requesting I be sent to a separation center for discharge. A small boat took me and my gear ashore, and I wound up in the base office. A chief told me to sit down. He took my letter and left. In a little while, he came back and told me the letter was made out wrong. I needed to go back to the ship and have it made out properly. Hitch—the ship had already sailed for the Canal. The chief told me to sit down and wait again. A while later, he came back and said the powers-that-be had decided to send me as a draft of one to Lido Beach, Long Island, for discharge.

On September 1, 1945, or thereabout, I was sent by train to Lido Beach, Long Island, New York for separation. The separation center was a large resort hotel, and the few days I spent there were very pleasant. The navy seemed to be trying to make up for three and a half years of disinterest. The Japanese officially surrendered on the Battleship Missouri on September 2nd.

I received my discharge on September 4, 1945. I put the ruptured duck badge [symbol of discharge] on my uniform and headed home to civilian life.

The USS LST-*388* After I Left

I RECEIVED A FEW LETTERS from shipmates after I left the ship, but over the years I lost contact with everyone.

USS *LST-388* passed through the Panama Canal and then sailed directly to Pearl Harbor. At Pearl Harbor, many in the crew became eligible for discharge. They returned to the States, to San Francisco, on the battleship USS *Arkansas*.

The Brodie Rig was removed from USS *LST-388*.

On July 3, 1946, the *New York Journal-American* printed a panoramic scene of the Bikini Atoll Lagoon, Marshall Islands, showing the many ships anchored, awaiting the July 1, 1946, atomic bomb test. Clearly in the front of the picture was the USS *LST-388*. The article stated fifty-nine ships felt the effect of the atom-bomb test. Three more were heavily damaged.

On September 3, 1946, I received a letter from Donald B. McKnight, my old communications officer. I think his feelings of the old USS *LST-388* represent all of us who served on her.

> I have often thought of the old 388 in the last six months. Perhaps you do not share my affection for the old tub, but I have often recalled with some sadness our days on that best of all LSTs. My last six months aboard her as skipper might have been pretty dismal had it not been for the help and support I got from the crew, but, with it, I don't know that I'll ever enjoy so rewarding an experience.

I learned from former shipmate Paul Roberts on May 2, 1989, that the USS *LST-388* was the mail ship during the Bikini Atom Bomb Test operation, and it survived the test.

According to a ship's record I received, the USS *LST-388* was towed to the state of Washington. She was decommissioned February 1, 1947, and struck from the navy list February 25, 1947. The report also said the ship was transferred to the US Maritime Administration and sold April 7, 1948.

But this may not be the true fate of USS *LST-388*, according to a *LST Scuttlebutt* (the official newsletter of the United States LST Association) article by Bob Reed. He reported that twenty-seven LSTs were sunk as target ships, and USS *LST-388* had been one of them.[20]

There may be some truth to this. In the June 1992 issue of *National Geographic* magazine, John L. Eliot wrote, in his article titled "In Bikini Lagoon, Life Thrives in a Nuclear Graveyard", ships that remained afloat or were salvaged after the atomic bomb test seethed with radiation. Improvised decontamination efforts failed. Most of these ships were towed 200 miles to Kwajalein. When further counter measures also failed, many derelicts were sunk in target practice off Kwajalein (Marshall Islands), Hawaii, and the US west coast.[21]

In 1984, I watched a television show featuring the famous stained-glass windows in the Washington National Cathedral, which contain a series of windows relating to events of World War II. One scene depicts an LST discharging a tank on the beach. I would like to think this is the USS *LST-388*.

THE USS *LST 388* AFTER I LEFT

Stained glass at the Washington National Cathedral.

Epilogue

AS I THINK BACK, I realize the war was a tragedy for members of my family and me. On my only thirty-day leave in June of 1945, I married Marge Ferenczi.

Marge and I had known each other all our lives, attended the same schools and church, but we did not date much before I joined the navy. I never went steady with a girl before dating her. While in the navy, I saw her only a few times before I went overseas, but I corresponded with her often.

The long periods on the ship were lonely times for me, and I longed to have a wife and my own home. It worried me to think of how I could support a wife and home. I seemed to have little inclination as to what direction to go in my life.

On my thirty-day leave in June 1945, I said to myself, "I will ask Marge to marry me, and together we will find a way to make a go of life." She said yes, and before my leave was up, we were married. The honeymoon at Lake George was a happy one.

After the war, we both worked. I returned to my pre-war job at Standard Oil Co. of New Jersey in the Marine Insurance Section, of the Marine Department at the RCA Building 30 Rockefeller Plaza. My pay was $35 a week—hardly enough to support a wife on. After about two years I felt I had to do something different. Besides the low pay, I found the job boring. The only thing interesting was observing the window washer as he hooked his belt to a bracket and stepped out. I could look down twenty-two stories and see him.

EPILOGUE

I did not use my G.I. Bill to go to college as I had become frustrated at NYU before the war. If I had not been married, I think I would have re-enlisted in the Navy.

I was raised during the Great Depression and saw and felt the problems of poverty for years on end. My grandfather Siemann (my mother's father) was a retired New York City Fireman. He had a steady income and helped us out when we needed it most. Security and a steady paycheck seemed so idealistic.

So, in 1947, I studied for, and passed the civil service tests, and, instead of a fireman, became a New York City patrolman. Children did not come along for five years. My daughter Lynn was born in 1950, and the following year, Marge gave birth to my son Carl. I thought we had an ideal family. We owned our home on Staten Island and had a summer cottage at Cranberry Lake, New Jersey.

When I was overseas, I had heard that Marge was dating a few men; one was a sea diver. I believe his name was Johnson. The seriousness of her relationship with this man dawned on me when, long after we married, I found stacks of letters from him tied with a ribbon. Why she didn't postpone marriage until she felt certain I was her choice, I'll never know.

After ten years of marriage, a lawyer called me at work and asked me to come to his office. I did, and he told me my wife wanted a divorce. Her reason—she just didn't love me. I had felt for some time that Marge was unhappy.

Marge and I obtained a legal separation rather than a divorce, but after trying to patch things up for almost four years, I gave up and we divorced.

Perhaps, without the war, Marge and I would have come to know each other better and never married. Why didn't I wait until after the war to get married? I never wanted to make anyone unhappy, but divorce is a difficult thing to overcome.

Although I provided child support, I saw little of my children as they grew up. Lynn and Carl were innocent victims of the war years, and that has always bothered me. Many war marriages floundered, tragedies by the score.

EPILOGUE

NYPD Sergeant Robert von der Osten.

In time, I moved on. A friend in the Police Department, Jim Fahy, invited me to a party at his house one night. I rang the doorbell at his home and a lady in a red velveteen dress came to the door. She looked just like Jim's wife, Willene. But it wasn't Willene, it was her twin sister, Earlene. We laughed about this then she turned to lead me up the stairs. Her red dress suited her, and as she walked up the stairs in front of me, I couldn't help but notice her shapely legs. Earlene had just moved to Staten Island from Alabama with her young daughter, Trudy. A divorce had her seeking a new start and she had moved to New York to be near her sister. I was glad she did.

EPILOGUE

Robert and Earlene's Wedding Day 1963.

I married Earlene Cynthia Jackson in 1963, and we had two children, Kurt and Barbara. I returned to college and earned my Bachelor's Degree from the John Jay College of Criminal Justice and eventually served as an instructor at the Police Academy.

After serving twenty years in the New York Police Department, I retired in 1968 and we moved to a small farm in Alabama, near my wife's parents. I taught school during the day and attended Jacksonville State University at night, earning my master's degree in Education. I also taught night classes in Police Science and other courses at Snead State Jr. College where Earlene worked in the Veterans Affairs Office.

EPILOGUE

My teaching days at Albertville High School in Alabama. I also taught classes at Snead State Jr. College in Boaz.

The next move came years later, in 1980, when we purchased a one-hundred-year-old house in Ormond Beach, Florida. We loved being so close to the beach. I never got tired of the ocean, and watching the boats go up and down the intracoastal waterway and out to sea.

Ormond Beach, FL—on the front porch with my father, Edwin, a WWI US Navy Gunners Mate. He passed away at the age of 93 shortly after this photo was taken.

EPILOGUE

(Above) My wife, Earlene, and I on our bikes in front of our 100-year-old house in Ormond Beach, Florida.

(Left) Our little cottage in the woods, Hayesville, North Carolina.

EPILOGUE

Attending a mock invasion on Jacksonville Beach, Florida with our youngest grandchildren, Anja and Kyler.

Our final move would come in 1996 when we made our way to the mountains of western North Carolina, to a small cottage in the town of Hayesville. Here I joined American Legion Post #532 and VFW Post #6812. We also became members of the Hayesville First United Methodist Church. Many of our happiest times have been spent here in this wonderful small town.

EPILOGUE

While in Washington, DC for the 1994 US LST Association convention, my wife and I visited our daughter Barbara who was living there at the time. She took us to Annapolis, Maryland to tour the United States Naval Academy. I had been here, aboard the brand-new USS *LST-388*, back in December 1942.

During my retirement years, Earlene and I attended several annual conventions of the United States LST Association, including ones held in San Diego, St. Louis, New Orleans, Pittsburg, and Washington, DC. At one such convention held in Chicago, in 1997, I, along with other D-Day veterans, were presented with a medal by a representative of the French government.

In 2001, the convention was held in Mobile, Alabama. A thrilling treat for us was a tour of the USS *LST-325*, found in Greece and sailed back to the United States by several of its original World War II crew. Just walking through the ship brought back so many memories. I was proud to show my wife and my youngest daughter, Barbara, the radio room and wheel house, where I had spent so much of my time.

My family and I also attended the convention in Norfolk, Virginia, in 2005. As part of the event, we were escorted to Little Creek, the amphibious base where I had trained so many years before when it was first being created. With all the modern ships, buildings, and conveniences there now, it was hard to believe it was the same place.

EPILOGUE

During the US LST Association Annual Convention in 2001, we traveled to Mobile, Alabama where the USS *LST-325* had been sailed to from Greece.

I doubted my son Kurt, daughters Barbara and Lynn, and grandsons Michael and Danny could imagine how the place looked during the time I trained there.

In June 2014, on the seventieth anniversary of D-Day at Normandy, the Rotary Club of Western North Carolina treated several of us to a trip to Bedford, Virginia, to attend a ceremony at the National D-Day Memorial there. My wife and I were driven to Asheville, North Carolina in a van, escorted by fellow veterans on motorcycles (the Patriot Guard Riders). The next day we boarded a bus, along with other Western North Carolina D-Day veterans, for the ride to Bedford.

We arrived in Bedford and toured the memorial the day before the ceremony. Much to my surprise, displayed on a concrete waterway, was the sculpture of the open bow and ramp of a landing craft. I'm proud to know our amphibious force, our LSTs, including the USS *LST-388*, will never be forgotten.

EPILOGUE

In the Radio Room of the USS *LST-325* during the 2001 US LST Association Convention in Mobile, Alabama.

EPILOGUE

USS *Tortuga* (LSD-46) Naval Amphibious Base, Little Creek, Virginia. This modern-day amphibious ship, referred to as a dock landing ship, or landing ship, dock is 610 ft. in length with a beam of 84 ft. outsizing the LSTs of WWII. The USS *LST-388* was 328 ft. with a beam of 50 ft.

Here I am onboard the USS *Tortuga* with two of my grandsons, Danny (l) and Michael (r). We were given a tour of the ship while attending the US LST Association Convention in Norfolk, VA in 2005. This was my first time back at Little Creek since my Amphibious Force training days in 1942.

EPILOGUE

Hayesville, NC—Memorial Day Service on the Square (2009) as part of VFW Post #6812 and American Legion Post #532.

Celebrating my 90th Birthday in St. Augustine, Florida with my four children: (l to r) Kurt, Lynn, Barbara and Carl (January 2010).

EPILOGUE

Attending my granddaughter Catherine's wedding in Jamaica in 2013. Left to right: Granddaughter Margaret, wife Earlene, Catherine (the bride), grandson Robert, myself, and daughter-in-law Maureen. This is my son Carl's family. Carl passed away in March of 2013.

EPILOGUE

Attending my youngest grandson Kyler's high school graduation in 2015. Left to right: My son Kurt, Earlene, Kyler, myself, and granddaughter Anja.

EPILOGUE

Above: In the lobby of Brasstown Valley Resort in Young Harris, GA on December 31, 2015

Right: Salute to the wife and family of Robert William von der Osten, December 8, 2016.

Below: Presentation of the flag to Robert's wife Earlene by active duty US Navy sailors at Robert's ceremony

May you have fair winds and following seas.

Robert William von der Osten
January 23, 1920 – December 3, 2016.

SEA FEVER
John Masefield

I must go down to the seas again,
To the lonely sea and the sky,
And all I ask is a tall ship
And a star to steer her by,
And the wheel's kick and the wind's song
And the white sails shaking
And a gray mist o the sea's face and a gray dawn breaking.

I must go down to the seas again,
For the call of the running tide
Is a wild call and a clear call
That may not be denied;
And all I ask is a windy day
With the white clouds flying,
And the flung spray and the blown spume,
And the seagulls crying.

I must go down to the seas again,
To the vagrant gypsy life.
To the gull's way and the whale's way
Where the wind's like a whetted knife;
And all I ask is a merry yarn
From a laughing fellow-rover,
And quiet sleep and a sweet dream
When the long trick's over.

I always loved this poem since learning it in grammar school. I can still hear my teacher recite it with expression, especially when she said, "where the wind's like a whetted knife." *—Robert von der Osten*

Sources—Reading List

Books

Churchill, Winston, *The Second World* War, Vol. IV: *Hinge of Fate*, Houghton Mifflin Company, Boston; Volume IV (1950), Cambridge, MA, pp. 109–111, pp. 118–119

Churchill, Winston, *The Second World* War, Vol. V: *Closing the Ring*, Houghton Mifflin, Boston, 1951.

Eisenhower, Dwight D., *Crusade in Europe*, Doubleday & Company, Inc., Garden City, New York, 1948

Hickey, Des and Smith, Gus. *Operation Avalanche: The Salerno Landings-1943*, McGraw-Hill Book Company, 1984

Morison, Samuel Eliot, *History of United States Naval Operations in World War II*, Volume II, *Operations in North African Waters, October 1942–June 1943*, Little, Brown and Company, Boston, 1959

Morison, Samuel Eliot, *History of United States Naval Operations in World War II*, Volume IX, *Sicily-Salerno-Anzio, January 1943–June 1944*, Little, Brown and Company, Boston, 1957

Morison, Samuel Eliot, *History of United States Naval Operations in World War II*, Volume XI, *The Invasion of France and Germany, 1944–1945*, Little, Brown and Company, Boston, 1959

Naval Institute Press, *Allied Landing Craft of World War Two*, Annapolis, MD, Fourth Printing, 1989

Norris, Eric, *Salerno: A Military Fiasco*, Stein and Day Publishers, New York,1983

Pyle, Ernie, *Brave Men*, Gosset & Dunlap, New York, 1945

Speer, Albert, *Inside the Third Reich Memoirs*, Translated from the German by Richard and Clara Winston, Bonanza Books, New York, 1982 (OR Macmillan Publishing Co., Inc., New York, 1970)

Building the Navy's Bases in World War II: History of the Bureau of Yards and Docks and the Civil Engineer Corps, 1940–1946, Volume 2, US Government Printing Office, 1947.

ARMY Green Book Series
U.S. Army in World War II

The Mediterranean Theater of Operations
Howe, George F., *Northwest Africa: Seizing the Initiative in the West*
Garland, LTC Albert N. and Smyth, Howard McGaw, *Sicily and the Surrender of Italy*
Blumenson, Martin, *Salerno to Cassino*

The European Theater of Operations
Harrison, Gordon A., *Cross-Channel Attack*, 1951

The Technical Services
The Medical Department: *Medical Service in the European Theater of Operations*
The Corps of Engineers: *The War Against Germany*
The Quartermaster Department: *Organization, Supply, and Services*, Volumes 1 and 2
The Quartermaster Department: *The Quartermaster Corps: Operations in the War Against Germany*
The Transportation Department: *Operations Overseas*

Endnotes

1. Winston Churchill, *The Hinge of Fate*. Houghton Mifflin C. 1950. Cambridge, MA, pp. 109–111, pp. 118–119.
2. Pyle, Ernie, *Brave Men*, Gosset & Dunlap, New York, 1945, p. 2.
3. Pyle, Ernie, *Brave Men*, Gosset & Dunlap, New York, 1945, p. 8.
4. Morison, Samuel Eliot, *History of United States Naval Operations in World War II*, Volume IX, *Sicily-Salerno-Anzio, January 1943–June 1944*, Little, Brown and Company, Boston, 1957, pg. 30–31.
5. Morison, Samuel Eliot, *History of United States Naval Operations in World War II*, Volume IX, *Sicily-Salerno-Anzio, January 1943–June 1944*, Little, Brown and Company, Boston, 1957, p. 32.
6. Morison, Samuel Eliot, *History of United States Naval Operations in World War II*, Volume IX, *Sicily-Salerno-Anzio, January 1943–June 1944*, Little, Brown and Company, Boston, 1957, pp. 107–108.
7. Morison, Samuel Eliot, *History of United States Naval Operations in World War II*, Volume IX, *Sicily-Salerno-Anzio, January 1943–June 1944*, Little, Brown and Company, Boston, 1957, pp. 120–121.
8. Churchill, Winston, *The Second World War, Closing the Ring*, Houghton Mifflin, Boston, 1951, pp. 27–28.
9. Morison, Samuel Eliot, *History of United States Naval Operations in World War II*, Volume IX, *Sicily-Salerno-Anzio, January 1943–June 1944*, Little, Brown and Company, Boston, 1957, p. 208.
10. Morison, Samuel Eliot, *History of United States Naval Operations in World War II*, Volume IX, *Sicily-Salerno-Anzio, January 1943–June 1944*, Little, Brown and Company, Boston, 1957, p. 260.
11. Morison, Samuel Eliot, *History of United States Naval Operations in World War II*, Volume IX, *Sicily-Salerno-Anzio, January 1943–June 1944*, Little, Brown and Company, Boston, 1957, p. 261.
12. Morison, Samuel Eliot, *History of United States Naval Operations in World War II*, Volume IX, *Sicily-Salerno-Anzio, January 1943–June 1944*, Little, Brown and Company, Boston, 1957, pp. 274–275.
13. Morison, Samuel Eliot, *History of United States Naval Operations in World War II*, Volume IX, *Sicily-Salerno-Anzio, January 1943–June 1944*, Little, Brown and Company, Boston, 1957, p.283.
14. From "The Luftwaffe's Fritz X Bomb at Salerno Was a Battleship Killer," John Laudermilk, in *World War II Magazine*, 5/90, Vol. 5, #1, May 1990. Empire Press, 602 S. King Street, Suite 300, Leesburg, VA 22075; pp. 12–16.

ENDNOTES

15. Churchill, Winston, *The Second World War, Closing the Ring*, Houghton Mifflin Company, Boston, 1951, p. 253.
16. Morison, Samuel Eliot, *History of United States Naval Operations in World War II*, Volume XI, *The Invasion of France and Germany, 1944–1945*, Little, Brown and Company, Boston, 1959. P. 63.
17. Morison, Samuel Eliot, *History of United States Naval Operations in World War II*, Volume XI, *The Invasion of France and Germany, 1944–1945*, Little, Brown and Company, Boston, 1959. P. 77.
18. Eisenhower, Dwight D., *Crusade in Europe*, Doubleday & Company, Inc., Garden City, New York, 1948, p. 322.
19. Holt, Corlis, When Disaster Struck, *VFW Magazine*, December 1988, p. 24.
20. Reed, Bob, Where Have All the LSTs Gone?, *LST Scuttlebutt*, January/February 1992, p. 29.
21. Eliot, John L., "In Bikini Lagoon Live Thrives in a Nuclear Graveyard," *National Geographic*, June 1992), pp. 70–83.

Photographs

MANY OF THE PHOTOS shared in this book come from the personal family collection of Robert von der Osten and from the personal family collection of William Schellhorn. All other photos, if not otherwise marked, are official Army or Navy photos in the public domain.

List of Maps

Maps were created specifically for this book by Jolan Falk of *Creative Force Maps*.

- Northeastern United States
- North Africa and the Mediterranean
- Invasion of Sicily
- Invasion of Salerno, Italy
- United Kingdom: England, Ireland and Wales
- Invasion of Normandy—France

Author Robert W. von der Osten, and his co-author and youngest daughter, Barbara von der Osten. (Photo taken January 2009)

About the Authors

Living on Staten Island, NY and commuting to work in Manhattan, **ROBERT W. VON DER OSTEN**, a second-generation German-American, struggled to find his place in the world. With the attack on Pearl Harbor, he soon found it with the United States Navy, serving in the newly created amphibious force, onboard the USS *LST-388*. Following the war, he served on the NYPD police force for twenty years, then as a high school and college instructor in Alabama. An armchair historian, von der Osten never forgot his WWII experiences, and continued to compile notes and articles to add to his war journals to eventually turn into his book, *LST-388*.

BARBARA VON DER OSTEN, an international traveler and scuba diver (and Robert's youngest daughter), earned her Bachelor's Degree in International Affairs at Florida State University and worked for a government consulting group in Washington, D.C. for several years. Tired of living inside the beltway, she eventually moved back to Florida. Her post-Washington, DC career has spanned various roles, from marketing specialist, to research analyst, to paralegal, yet writing is her first love and one she has finally returned to.